SOURCES OF CIVILIZATION IN THE WEST

Robert Lee Wolff, *General Editor*

ERICH S. GRUEN, the editor of this volume, is Associate Professor of History at the University of California, Berkeley. He is a Guggenheim Fellow for 1969–70, and the author of *Roman Politics and the Criminal Courts,* as well as several articles and reviews in the field of classical history.

ALREADY PUBLISHED

The Age of Imperialism, *edited by Robin W. Winks,* S-205

The Ancient World: Justice, Heroism, and Responsibility, *edited by Zeph Stewart,* S-141

Century of Genius: European Thought 1600–1700, *edited by Richard T. Vann,* S-149

The Conversion of Western Europe, 350–750, *edited by J. N. Hillgarth,* S-203

The Crisis of Church & State, 1050–1300, *by Brian Tierney (with selected documents),* S-102

The English Reform Tradition, 1790–1910, *edited by Sydney W. Jackman,* S-120

The Enlightenment, *edited by Frank E. Manuel,* S-121

The French Revolution, *edited by Philip Dawson,* S-161

Icon and Minaret: Sources of Byzantine and Islamic Civilization, *edited by Charles M. Brand,* S-199

The Image of Rome, *edited by Erich S. Gruen,* S-194

The Italian Renaissance, *edited by Werner L. Gundersheimer,* S-128

Nineteenth-Century Thought: The Discovery of Change, *edited by Richard L. Schoenwald,* S-129

The Protestant Reformation, *edited by Lewis W. Spitz,* S-140

THE IMAGE
OF ROME

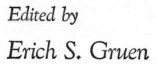

Edited by

Erich S. Gruen

PRENTICE-HALL, INC.
Englewood Cliffs, New Jersey

A SPECTRUM BOOK

Current printing (last number):

10 9 8 7 6 5 4 3 2 1

PRENTICE-HALL INTERNATIONAL, INC. (*London*)
PRENTICE-HALL OF AUSTRALIA, PTY. LTD. (*Sydney*)
PRENTICE-HALL OF CANADA, LTD. (*Toronto*)
PRENTICE-HALL OF INDIA PRIVATE LIMITED (*New Delhi*)
PRENTICE-HALL OF JAPAN, INC. (*Tokyo*)

FOREWORD

To make from Roman authors a selection of excerpts that will convey to a modern reader in the words of the Romans themselves an adequate picture of Roman society over a period of eleven hundred years is a challenging task indeed. From relatively primitive beginnings as an Italian settlement, not marked out by any apparent natural advantages to outstrip its neighboring villages, Rome moved first to the consolidation of its own region, then to the conquest of Italy, and eventually to that of Greece, the Eastern Mediterranean, and of virtually the whole of Western Europe and North Africa. Its early republican institutions, strained by the acquisition of vast territories, gave way to those perhaps more suitable to governing an empire. Its civilization, its laws, its monuments extend from the borders of Scotland to those of Persia.

This astonishing achievement has often blinded its students to the fact that Romans were as diverse in their views as modern men, and that the peoples they conquered responded as individuals diversely to the conquest. By centering this collection of original materials around the diverse views—both positive and negative—of immediate contemporaries, Professor Gruen has succeeded in conveying the complexity of Rome's development. He has made skillful use of the surviving texts that reveal the doubts of Romans and the resentments of their victims—texts that are often obscure and little known compared to the famous words of praise for Roman achievement that we find in Cicero and Virgil. But of course, Cicero and Virgil are here too.

By limiting the number of his sources, by providing rather extensive excerpts from each, by supplying succinct but ample commentary on the course of Roman development and on the character and ideas of each of his Roman authorities, Professor Gruen has managed to take us triumphantly from the primitive beginnings through the conquests that made the Empire, and from the con-

stitution of the Republic to its transformation in the new era of
Augustus, to its miseries in the first and its glories in the second
century of the Empire, and to the eventual fading of its ideal. He
has done this so unobtrusively that some students may not recognize
what a *tour de force* he has performed.

Robert Lee Wolff
Archibald Cary Coolidge
Professor of History
Harvard University

CONTENTS

Introduction   1

I. ROME THE CONQUEROR   3

Ennius: The *Annales, 4* Polybius: *Histories, 9* Cicero: *On the
Consular Provinces, 18* Cato: *On the Rhodian War, 22* Sallust:
Letter of Mithridates, 25

II. THE REPUBLICAN CONSTITUTION   30

Cicero: *On the State, 31* Sallust: *The Conspiracy of Catiline, 41*

III. THE NEW ERA   52

Augustus: *Achievements of the Divine Augustus, 54* Vergil: The
Fourth Eclogue and the *Aeneid, 58* Horace: *Odes, 65* The
Pumpkinification of Claudius, 75 Lucan: *Pharsalia, 85*

IV. THE GROWTH OF MONARCHY   92

Pliny: *Panegyric to Trajan, 94* Marcus Aurelius: *Meditations, 99*
Dio Cassius: The Advantage of Monarchy, *110* Tacitus: *Dialogue on Orators, 112* Juvenal: *Fourth Satire, 118*

V. THE EMPIRE AND ITS SUBJECTS   127

Claudius: *Speech on Gallic Senators, 129* Tacitus: *Annals, 132*
Josephus: *The Jewish War, 135* Aelius Aristides: *Oration to
Rome, 141* *Acts of the Pagan Martyrs, 149* The *Sibylline Or-
acles, 154* Tacitus: *The Histories, 160*

VI. THE FADED IDEAL   165

Ammianus Marcellinus: *History, 166*

vii

Introduction

The "grandeur of Rome" is a phrase familiar from textbooks and anthologies. Rome's achievement and her legacy continue to be celebrated. The images (or the stereotypes) conjured up by the word "Roman" are imposing: law and ordered government, disciplined legions, roads, aqueducts, monumental arches, engineering feats—the noble and dedicated Roman. It is not the modern world which created those images. Roman writers, thinkers, and propagandists perpetrated and fostered them. How far the ideals approximated to reality is not always easy to discern—and perhaps it does not matter much. As any student of Freud and Sorel will know, myths can be more potent than realities. The purpose of this book is to illustrate, through a number of selections, what the Romans thought of themselves, or (perhaps more accurately) how they liked to see themselves. Our own views, inescapably, are very much shaped by the nature of the surviving testimony. And that testimony, in most instances, was produced by Romans, or by men who received their inspiration in and from Rome. The pictures which they conveyed (consciously or unconsciously) were those which Rome sought to have transmitted to her own people and to the outside world. There was little encouragement for the works of men who challenged Rome, her motives, and her ideals. The imbalance is reflected in the literature preserved from antiquity. But the voices of Rome's enemies and critics are not altogether silent. They include disgruntled politicians, satirists, provincials, and religious minorities. In these pages, authors who present the enthusiastic and familiar portraits will be juxtaposed to more sobering reflections by Romans or provincials who provide the other side of the story.

Rome's portrait will be examined from various angles. The robust image of the conqueror, vaunting her martial glory and her triumphs, appears frequently in the literature. Rome subdued the rude barbarian and extended the boundaries of civilization to the ends of the world, so her admirers exclaimed. Those who succumbed to Roman power did not always agree; and they too had their

1

spokesmen. The Republican constitution was regarded as a model of balance and harmony; excessive power was limited by institutional checks; the wise governed in the interests of the lowly; all classes cooperated in the spirit of community. Writers and thinkers saw the constitution as fulfilling all the principles of Greek political theory. But some could see the darker side: principles and schemata did not reflect the corruption and selfishness of the ruling class or the oppression of the commons. The discrepancy between ideals and realities helped precipitate civil war and the fall of the Republic. When a new order emerged, a similar pattern can be discerned. Eulogy and panegyric greeted the Augustan system: the monarchical empire had brought peace and prosperity. But the passage of time brought disillusionment. Rulers could become tyrants or fools. Literature produced by critics of the early empire survives on record. Greater maturity and stability followed in the age of the Antonines. A noble pattern informed the practices of the emperors. They were to be constitutional monarchs, shepherds of the people, dispensers of justice and equality. The subject populace of the empire was to be raised on a level with Romans and Italians. Universal citizenship brought unity and common purpose. But even in the Antonine age discontent received expression. It came from Romans for whom the price paid by freedom for security was too high; and it came also from provincials and from racial and religious minorities who did not benefit from the "blessings of empire.

There is an inevitable element of artificiality (not to say subjectivity) in any collection of edited excerpts. Hence, it has been thought advisable to include selections only from contemporary authors, in the strictest sense. For example, despite the literary merits and importance of his work, Livy has not been used for Rome's wars of expansion since he did not live through them; Ennius and Polybius are better guides to the feelings of Romans who experienced that era directly. If Lucan and Tacitus are quoted for periods earlier than their own, it is only when they are consciously employing their material to criticize their contemporary circumstances. Some of the selections are short fragments, others are lengthier disquisitions. But the central theme runs throughout: a counterpoint between image and reality, between patriotic glorification and dissent.

Part One

 ROME THE CONQUEROR

The Roman empire was not created overnight. Centuries of almost continuous warfare consumed Roman energies and resources. The Italian peninsula belonged to Rome by the mid-third century B.C., but expansion, without cease, continued against foreign foes in the western and eastern Mediterranean. The great era of Roman imperialism encompassed the years 264 to 146 B.C., when Sicily, Sardinia, Spain, North Africa, Greece, Macedon, the Aegean, and Asia Minor methodically fell under Roman sway. Rome's military machine had already eclipsed the achievements of all previous imperial states. And the job was continued a century later when Pompey's conquests converted the eastern monarchies into Roman provinces and Julius Caesar reduced the whole of Gaul and penetrated even into Britain.

Whether or not the Romans enjoyed war, they lived with it—and almost incessantly. There is no mistaking the exhilaration and pride in the steady march of Roman arms which is reflected by the literature. Nor was it native-born Romans alone who heaped praise on the state and gloried in its expansion. Ennius came out of a Greek literary tradition in southern Italy to celebrate Roman exploits in epic poetry. Polybius was a Greek statesman, as well as an historian, who wrote his work in Rome, a work filled with admiration for the Roman achievement. Both men lived through that concentrated burst of activity which left Rome without a challenger in the Mediterranean world. Training, discipline, and doggedness in war; patriotism and respect for

antique traditions at home: these were the qualities stressed by
Ennius and Polybius, the qualities that brought empire. The scale
of Rome's conquests, the superiority of her accomplishment over
previous imperial powers, and the character of the people who
brought it about left a profound impression upon contemporary
observers. Three quarters of a century later, Cicero could boast
in similar terms of new Roman conquests in the east and in Gaul.
There is the same unabashed pride in sheer extension of territory
and growth of Roman suzerainty. Foreign foes are humbled and
subjects rejoice in Roman rule. Success demonstrated virtue and
called for more of the same. Such was the prevailing attitude
throughout the era of the Republic.

But not all Romans could be persuaded to endorse that philosophy. Even in that age of exuberance and unchecked expansionism
there were statesmen who objected. In the mid-second century
Cato the Elder warned of overweening arrogance which promoted
war for its own sake on the flimsiest of pretexts. Conquests could
have their own ill effects on Roman character. By the end of the
Republic, Sallust documented those ill effects in ruthless detail.
He provides a sharp antidote to Cicero's bluster. The victims of
Roman aggression could use a spokesman. Sallust puts into the
mouth of Mithridates the bitter response of Rome's enemies to her
aggrandizement and greed. The selections included here provide, so far as the nature of our evidence allows, both sides of
the coin on Roman imperialism.

Ennius: The *Annales*

Quintus Ennius (239–169 B.C.) stands near the beginnings
of Latin literature. But "beginnings" is a term dependent
upon the accidents of transmission. A prior tradition is
lost. Like the Homeric poems in Greece, Ennius already
shows mastery of the epic poetic form. An Italian from
Calabria, he grew up in those portions of Italy which had
been colonized by Greece and where Hellenic influences were
strong. Homer was his literary model and Homeric touches

can be found throughout the *Annales*. But Ennius was also a soldier in Rome's armies and was patronized by Roman aristocrats in the capital. He experienced at firsthand that heady period when Rome burst the confines of Italy and extended her hegemony without serious setback through much of the Mediterranean. When he produced an epic, he chose as a theme not distant mythology but the history of Rome to his own day, set out in poetic form. Martial valor and dedication to the state are the values that he celebrates, thereby stamping an indelible image upon Roman character which his contemporaries and successors perpetuated. The *Annales* of Ennius carried a powerful impact. Roman schoolboys memorized his verses, poets like Lucretius and Vergil sang his praises and emulated his techniques many generations later. The poem itself is no longer extant in its complete or continuous form. But later quotations were numerous and have preserved over 600 lines. The selections included here are fragments; they cannot, therefore, give continuity or narrative. But they give the robust and masculine flavor of his lines. They illustrate those vigorous qualities which Romans preferred to see in their ancestors and in themselves.

The following selections are from Ennius, *Annales*, fragments 181–550 (with omissions), trans. E. H. Warmington in *Remains of Old Latin*, I (Cambridge, Mass.: Harvard University Press, 1967), 71–207, *passim*. Reprinted by permission of the publishers and *The Loeb Classical Library*.

Then strode they through tall timber-trees and hewed
With hatchets; mighty oaks they overset;
Down crashed the holm and shivered ash outhacked;
Felled was the lofty fir; they wrenched right down
Tall towering pines; and every woody tree
In frondent forest rang and roared and rustled.

"Ye gods, hear this my prayer a little while: just as from my body I breathe my last for the Roman people's sake, with foreknowledge and awareness, in arms and in battle,

Not always does Jupiter upset your plans; now he stands on our side.

To men of fortitude is fortune granted.

The bristling spears of the warriors crowded thick upon the plain.

The line of lancers scattered its lances; came a rain-storm of iron.

These the Poeni houghed, wicked haughty foes.

They gave chase: with mightiest clatter their hoofs shook the ground.

"Many things does one day bring about in war . . . and many fortunes through chance sink low again. In no wise has fortune followed any man all his days.

The soldiers struggled with sturdy strength.

Go on, O Muse, to tell what each commander of the Romans wrought with his troops in war with King Philip.

He was watching the mettle of his army, waiting to see if they would grumble, saying "what rest will there be at last from our fighting, or end to our hard toil?"

The commander . . . cheers and cheers them on

Then he led some eight thousand warriors, wearing badges, chosen men, strong to bear war well.

Says he, "Give them destruction, Jupiter, with utter hell!"

Then the round shields resounded, and the iron spear-points whizzed;

and the spear, shot into his breast, whizzed as it sped through.

> One man by his delays restored the state;
> Hearsay he would not put before our safety;

Hence to this day the warrior's glory shines—
In after time, and more than it shone once.

Yes, all those victors, every single soul,
Contented from the bottom of their hearts—
Sleep on a sudden, over all the plain,
Most soft thrilled tingling through them, tended well
By wine.

"It is the part of commanders who are men of deeds, to keep discipline.

"in the place where my very duty displays itself and commands me.

From all sides the javelins like a rain-storm showered in upon the tribune, and pierced his buckler; then jangled the embossment under spears, the helmet too with brassy clang; but not one of them, though strain they did from every side, could rend apart his body with the iron. Every time he shakes and breaks the waves of lances; sweat covers all his body; he is hard distressed; to breathe he has not a chance. The iron came flying as the Histrians cast the spears from their hands to harass him.

He tumbled and withal his armour dinned over him.

The horsemen charged, and the beating of their hollow hoofs shook the ground.

They rushed together as when the breath of the showery Wind of the South and the Wind of the North with his counterblast strive to upheave billows on the mighty main.

Uproars to heaven the shout that rose from either side.

No, it is not meet that good warriors should mumble; warriors who, straining in the toil of battle-fields, have given birth to deeds.

nor do their firm bodies languish at all.

when the sunny days shall make them lengthen long.

On manners and on men of good old time
Stands firm the Roman State.

Brave are the Romans as the sky's profound

When the commander sets forth with his hosts,

Nor any fear holds them; trusting in their valiance, they rest.

"He who has conquered is not conqueror
Unless the conquered one confesses it"

The best youth of Rome with fine spirit

Sword-girt and slender round the waist.

girt round their hearts with broadswords.

and the light-armed followed in lances.

The skirmishers, holding broad cutting-spears, advanced in a body.

. . . which come sturdily; the fire-spear was hurled

Blunted back were spears that clashed against oncoming spears

And when his head was falling, the trumpet finished alone its tune; and even as the warrior did perish, a hoarse blare sped from the brass.

Hereupon foot pressed foot and weapons weapons rubbed, and warrior warrior thronged.

Here now our men gave way a little while.

"Whither go you all so rashly?

Order was given to stand and delve into their bodies with spears.

Let chariots of wrathfulness loose like a flood.

Polybius: *Histories*

Foreign conquests meant spoils. The Roman treasury swelled and the list of captives lengthened. But tangible results went beyond material items. Among the Greek leaders shipped to Rome as hostages for the good behavior of their countrymen was the Achaean politician and intellectual Polybius (ca. 208–126 B.C.). His sojourn in Rome proved of tremendous benefit for himself and for the city. Polybius joined the intellectual circle of some of Rome's leading aristocrats and most influential politicians. Practical experience in Greek government was combined with direct contact with the men who made Roman policy. Polybius had the advantage of observing operations from the inside in Rome without the responsibility of making decisions. Hence came the leisure time to record his observations and construct a history of his age. He drew on the lengthy Hellenistic historiographical tradition but added the insight of the practical and practiced statesman. Polybius recognized fully that he had witnessed a remarkable age. His purpose was to demonstrate the manner in which Rome had subdued much of the known world and to examine the institutions and men who had made it possible. The passages reproduced here show Polybius' admiration for a city-state which had far outstripped the achievements of previous empires. Part of the reason, in his view, is respect for tradition, conscious glorification and emulation of ancestors, and a firm sense of submitting individual claims to the service of state. Rome's success was due not just to military valor and skill, but to a system of institutions which bound her citizens together, commanding their loyalty and inspiring their confidence. The powerful picture, drawn, as it was, by a Greek and read by Greek and Roman alike, became compelling.

The following selections are from Polybius, *Histories,* Book I, Secs. 1–2; Book III, Secs. 1–4; Book VI, Secs. 52–54, 58; trans. Evelyn S. Shuckburgh in *The Histories of Polybius,* I (London and New York: Macmillan and Co., 1889), 1–2, 166–70, 502–4, 507–8.

1. Had the praise of History been passed over by former Chroniclers it would perhaps have been incumbent upon me to urge the choice and special study of records of this sort, as the readiest means men can have of correcting their knowledge of the past. But my predecessors have not been sparing in this respect. They have all begun and ended, so to speak, by enlarging on this theme: asserting again and again that the study of History is in the truest sense an education, and a training for political life; and that the most instructive, or rather the only, method of learning to bear with dignity the vicissitudes of fortune is to recall the catastrophes of others. It is evident, therefore, that no one need think it his duty to repeat what has been said by many, and said well. Least of all myself: for the surprising nature of the events which I have undertaken to relate is in itself sufficient to challenge and stimulate the attention of every one, old or young, to the study of my work. Can any one be so indifferent or idle as not to care to know by what means, and under what kind of polity, almost the whole inhabited world was conquered and brought under the dominion of the single city of Rome, and that too within a period of not quite fifty-three years? Or who again can be so completely absorbed in other subjects of contemplation or study, as to think any of them superior in importance to the accurate understanding of an event for which the past affords no precedent.

2. We shall best show how marvellous and vast our subject is by comparing the most famous Empires which preceded, and which have been the favourite themes of historians, and measuring them with the superior greatness of Rome. There are but three that deserve even to be so compared and measured: and they are these. The Persians for a certain length of time were possessed of a great empire and dominion. But every time they ventured beyond the limits of Asia, they found not only their empire, but their own existence also in danger. The Lacedaemonians, after contending for supremacy in Greece for many generations, when

they did get it, held it without dispute for barely twelve years.
The Macedonians obtained dominion in Europe from the lands
bordering on the Adriatic to the Danube,—which after all is but
a small fraction of this continent,—and, by the destruction of
the Persian Empire, they afterwards added to that the dominion
of Asia. And yet, though they had the credit of having made
themselves masters of a larger number of countries and states than
any people had ever done, they still left the greater half of the
inhabited world in the hands of others. They never so much as
thought of attempting Sicily, Sardinia, or Libya: and as to Europe,
to speak the plain truth, they never even knew of the most warlike tribes of the West. The Roman conquest, on the other hand,
was not partial. Nearly the whole inhabited world was reduced
by them to obedience: and they left behind them an empire not
to be paralleled in the past or rivalled in the future. Students will
gain from my narrative a clearer view of the whole story, and of
the numerous and important advantages which such exact record
of events offers.

*   *   *

1. I stated in my first book that my work was to start from the
Social war, the Hannibalian war, and the war for the possession
of Coele-Syria. In the same book I stated my reasons for devoting
my first two books to a sketch of the period preceding those
events. I will now, after a few prefatory remarks as to the scope
of my own work, address myself to giving a complete account of
these wars, the causes which led to them, and which account for
the proportions to which they attained.

The one aim and object, then, of all that I have undertaken
to write is to show how, when, and why all the known parts of
the world fell under the dominion of Rome. Now as this great
event admits of being exactly dated as to its beginning, duration,
and final accomplishment, I think it will be advantageous to give,
by way of preface, a summary statement of the most important
phases in it between the beginning and the end. For I think I
shall thus best secure to the student an adequate idea of my whole
plan; for as the comprehension of the whole is a help to the
understanding of details, and the knowledge of details of great
service to the clear conception of the whole; believing that the

best and clearest knowledge is that which is obtained from a combination of these, I will preface my whole history by a brief summary of its contents.

I have already described its scope and limits. As to its several parts, the first consists of the above mentioned wars, while the conclusion or closing scene is the fall of the Macedonian monarchy. The time included between these limits is fifty-three years; and never has an equal space embraced events of such magnitude and importance. In describing them I shall start from the 140th Olympiad and shall arrange my exposition in the following order:

2. First I shall indicate the causes of the Punic or Hannibalian war: and shall have to describe how the Carthaginians entered Italy; broke up the Roman power there; made the Romans tremble for their safety and the very soil of their country; and contrary to all calculation acquired a good prospect of surprising Rome itself.

I shall next try to make it clear how in the same period Philip of Macedon, after finishing his war with the Aetolians, and subsequently settling the affairs of Greece, entered upon a design of forming an offensive and defensive alliance with Carthage.

Then I shall tell how Antiochus and Ptolemy Philopator first quarrelled and finally went to war with each other for the possession of Coele-Syria.

Next how the Rhodians and Prusias went to war with the Byzantines, and compelled them to desist from exacting dues from ships sailing into the Pontus.

At this point I shall pause in my narrative to introduce a disquisition upon the Roman Constitution, in which I shall show that its peculiar character contributed largely to their success, not only in reducing all Italy to their authority, and in acquiring a supremacy over the Iberians and Gauls besides, but also at last, after their conquest of Carthage, to their conceiving the idea of universal dominion.

Along with this I shall introduce another digression on the fall of Hiero of Syracuse.

After these digressions will come the disturbances in Egypt; how, after the death of King Ptolemy, Antiochus and Philip entered into a compact for the partition of the dominions of that monarch's infant son. I shall describe their treacherous dealings,

Philip laying hands upon the islands of the Aegean, and Caria and Samos, Antiochus upon Coele-Syria and Phoenicia.

3. Next, after a summary recapitulation of the proceedings of the Carthaginians and Romans in Iberia, Libya, and Sicily, I shall, following the changes of events, shift the scene of my story entirely to Greece. Here I shall first describe the naval battles of Attalus and the Rhodians against Philip; and the war between Philip and Rome, the persons engaged, its circumstances and result.

Next to this I shall have to record the wrath of the Aetolians, in consequence of which they invited the aid of Antiochus, and thereby gave rise to what is called the Asiatic war against Rome and the Achaean league. Having stated the causes of this war, and described the crossing of Antiochus into Europe, I shall have to show first in what manner he was driven from Greece; secondly, how, being defeated in the war, he was forced to cede all his territory west of Taurus; and thirdly, how the Romans, after crushing the insolence of the Gauls, secured undisputed possession of Asia, and freed all the nations on the west of Taurus from the fear of barbarian inroads and the lawless violence of the Gauls.

Next, after reviewing the disasters of the Aetolians and Cephallenians, I shall pass to the wars waged by Eumenes against Prusias and the Gauls; as well as that carried on in alliance with Ariarathes against Pharnaces.

Finally, after speaking of the unity and settlement of the Peloponnese, and of the growth of the commonwealth of Rhodes, I shall add a summary of my whole work, concluding by an account of the expedition of Antiochus Epiphanes against Egypt; of the war against Perseus; and the destruction of the Macedonian monarchy. Throughout the whole narrative it will be shown how the policy adopted by the Romans in one after another of these cases, as they arose, led to their eventual conquest of the whole world.

4. And if our judgment of individuals and constitutions, for praise or blame, could be adequately formed from a simple consideration of their successes or defeats, I must necessarily have stopped at this point, and have concluded my history as soon as I reached these last events in accordance with my original plan. For at this point the fifty-three years were coming to an end, and the

progress of the Roman power had arrived at its consummation. And, besides, by this time the acknowledgment had been extorted from all that the supremacy of Rome must be accepted, and her commands obeyed. But in truth, judgments of either side founded on the bare facts of success or failure in the field are by no means final. It has often happened that what seemed the most signal successes have, from ill management, brought the most crushing disasters in their train; while not unfrequently the most terrible calamities, sustained with spirit, have been turned to actual advantage. I am bound, therefore, to add to my statement of facts a discussion on the subsequent policy of the conquerors, and their administration of their universal dominion: and again on the various feelings and opinions entertained by other nations towards their rulers. And I must also describe the tastes and aims of the several nations, whether in their private lives or public policy. The present generation will learn from this whether they should shun or seek the rule of Rome; and future generations will be taught whether to praise and imitate, or to decry it. The usefulness of my history, whether for the present or the future, will mainly lie in this. For the end of a policy should not be, in the eyes either of the actors or their historians, simply to conquer others and bring all into subjection. Nor does any man of sense go to war with his neighbours for the mere purpose of mastering his opponents; nor go to sea for the mere sake of the voyage; nor engage in professions and trades for the sole purpose of learning them. In all these cases the objects are invariably the pleasure, honour, or profit which are the results of the several employments. Accordingly the object of this work shall be to ascertain exactly what the position of the several states was, after the universal conquest by which they fell under the power of Rome, until the commotions and disturbances which broke out at a later period. These I designed to make the starting-point of what may almost be called a new work, partly because of the greatness and surprising nature of the events themselves, but chiefly because, in the case of most of them, I was not only an eye-witness, but in some cases one of the actors, and in others the chief director.

*　　　　*　　　　*

52. If we look however at separate details, for instance at the provisions for carrying on a war, we shall find that whereas for a

naval expedition the Carthaginians are the better trained and prepared,—as it is only natural with a people with whom it has been hereditary for many generations to practise this craft, and to follow the seaman's trade above all nations in the world,—yet, in regard to military service on land, the Romans train themselves to a much higher pitch than the Carthaginians. The former bestow their whole attention upon this department: whereas the Carthaginians wholly neglect their infantry, though they do take some slight interest in the cavalry. The reason of this is that they employ foreign mercenaries, the Romans native and citizen levies. It is in this point that the latter polity is preferable to the former. They have their hopes of freedom ever resting on the courage of mercenary troops: the Romans on the valour of their own citizens and the aid of their allies. The result is that even if the Romans have suffered a defeat at first, they renew the war with undiminished forces, which the Carthaginians cannot do. For, as the Romans are fighting for country and children, it is impossible for them to relax the fury of their struggle; but they persist with obstinate resolution until they have overcome their enemies. What has happened in regard to their navy is an instance in point. In skill the Romans are much behind the Carthaginians, as I have already said; yet the upshot of the whole naval war has been a decided triumph for the Romans, owing to the valour of their men. For although nautical science contributes largely to success in seafights, still it is the courage of the marines that turns the scale most decisively in favour of victory. The fact is that Italians as a nation are by nature superior to Phoenicians and Libyans both in physical strength and courage; but still their habits also do much to inspire the youth with enthusiasm for such exploits. One example will be sufficient of the pains taken by the Roman state to turn out men ready to endure anything to win a reputation in their country for valour.

53. Whenever one of their illustrious men dies, in the course of his funeral, the body with all its paraphernalia is carried into the forum to the Rostra, as a raised platform there is called, and sometimes is propped upright upon it so as to be conspicuous, or, more rarely, is laid upon it. Then with all the people standing round, his son, if he has left one of full age and he is there, or, failing him, one of his relations, mounts the Rostra and delivers a speech concerning the virtues of the deceased, and the successful exploits

performed by him in his lifetime. By these means the people are reminded of what has been done, and made to see it with their own eyes,—not only such as were engaged in the actual transactions but those also who were not;—and their sympathies are so deeply moved, that the loss appears not to be confined to the actual mourners, but to be a public one affecting the whole people. After the burial and all the usual ceremonies have been performed, they place the likeness of the deceased in the most conspicuous spot in his house, surmounted by a wooden canopy or shrine. This likeness consists of a mask made to represent the deceased with extraordinary fidelity both in shape and colour. These likenesses they display at public sacrifices adorned with much care. And when any illustrious member of the family dies, they carry these masks to the funeral, putting them on men whom they thought as like the originals as possible in height and other personal peculiarities. And these substitutes assume clothes according to the rank of the person represented: if he was a consul or praetor, a toga with purple stripes; if a censor, whole purple; if he had also celebrated a triumph or performed any exploit of that kind, a toga embroidered with gold. These representatives also ride themselves in chariots, while the fasces and axes, and all the other customary insignia of the particular offices, lead the way, according to the dignity of the rank in the state enjoyed by the deceased in his lifetime; and on arriving at the Rostra they all take their seats on ivory chairs in their order. There could not easily be a more inspiring spectacle than this for a young man of noble ambitions and virtuous aspirations. For can we conceive any one to be unmoved at the sight of all the likenesses collected together of the men who have earned glory, all as it were living and breathing? Or what could be a more glorious spectacle?

54. Besides the speaker over the body about to be buried, after having finished the panegyric of this particular person, starts upon the others whose representatives are present, beginning with the most ancient, and recounts the successes and achievements of each. By this means the glorious memory of brave men is continually renewed; the fame of those who have performed any noble deed is never allowed to die; and the renown of those who have done good service to their country becomes a matter of common knowledge to the multitude, and part of the heritage of posterity. But the chief benefit of the ceremony is that it inspires young men to

shrink from no exertion for the general welfare, in the hope of obtaining the glory which awaits the brave. And what I say is confirmed by this fact. Many Romans have volunteered to decide a whole battle by single combat; not a few have deliberately accepted certain death, some in time of war to secure the safety of the rest, some in time of peace to preserve the safety of the commonwealth. There have also been instances of men in office putting their own sons to death, in defiance of every custom and law, because they rated the interests of their country higher than those of natural ties even with their nearest and dearest. There are many stories of this kind, related of many men in Roman history; but one will be enough for our present purpose; and I will give the name as an instance to prove the truth of my words.

*   *   *

58. Resuming my history from the point at which I started on this digression I will briefly refer to one transaction, that I may give a practical illustration of the perfection and power of the Roman polity at that period, as though I were producing one of his works as a specimen of the skill of a good artist.

When Hannibal, after conquering the Romans in the battle at Cannae, got possession of the eight thousand who were guarding the Roman camp, he made them all prisoners of war, and granted them permission to send messages to their relations that they might be ransomed and return home. They accordingly selected ten of their chief men, whom Hannibal allowed to depart after binding them with an oath to return. But one of them, just as he had got outside the palisade of the camp, saying that he had forgotten something, went back; and, having got what he had left behind, once more set out, under the belief that by means of this return he had kept his promise and discharged his oath. Upon the arrival of the envoys at Rome, imploring and beseeching the Senate not to grudge the captured troops their return home, but to allow them to rejoin their friends by paying three minae each for them, —for these were the terms, they said, granted by Hannibal,—and declaring that the men deserved redemption, for they had neither played the coward in the field, nor done anything unworthy of Rome, but had been left behind to guard the camp; and that, when all the rest had perished, they had yielded to absolute necessity in surrendering to Hannibal: though the Romans had been severely defeated in the battles, and though they were at the time deprived of, roughly speaking, all their allies, they neither yielded so far to misfortune as to disregard what was becoming to themselves, nor omitted to take into account any necessary consideration. They saw through Hannibal's purpose in thus acting,—which was at once to get a large supply of money, and at the same time to take away all enthusiasm from the troops opposed to him, by showing that even the conquered had a hope of getting safe home again. Therefore the Senate, far from acceding to the request, refused all pity even to their own relations, and disregarded the services to be expected from these men in the future: and thus frustrated Hannibal's calculations, and the hopes which he had founded on these prisoners, by refusing to ransom them; and at the same time established the rule for their own men, that they must either conquer or die on the field, as there was no other hope of safety for them if they were beaten. With this answer they dismissed the nine envoys who returned of their own accord; but the tenth who had put the cunning trick in practice for discharging himself of his oath they put in chains and delivered to the enemy. So that Hannibal was not so much rejoiced at his victory in the battle, as struck with astonishment at the unshaken firmness and lofty spirit displayed in the resolutions of these senators.

Cicero: On the Consular Provinces

By 146 B.C. Rome had removed all serious challengers to her supremacy. For three quarters of a century she consolidated her gains and eschewed further territorial acquisition. But renewed activity was spurred by the aggressions of Mithridates, king of Pontus in Asia Minor. Pompey the Great completed a major campaign in the east in 62 B.C., adding new provinces and subject dependencies. Four years later Julius Caesar embarked on his famed venture in Gaul which was to bring Roman boundaries all the way to the Rhine and to the English Channel. The martial spirit was again intoned by Roman spokesmen. Nor was it military men alone who hymned the praises of the conqueror. Mar-

cus Tullius Cicero (106–43 B.C.) was pre-eminently a man of
peace who shunned arms whenever possible. But the fiery
rhetoric of his oratory could also play on patriotic sentiments. In 56 B.C. a movement was stirred to recall Caesar
from his post in Gaul. This was not an effort to check
aggrandizement but simply a political move to insert a new
commander. Cicero's speech, *De Provinciis Consularibus* (*On
the Consular Provinces*), was a ringing defense of Caesar's
achievements. It also contains a classic defense of Roman
imperialism. All neighbors are potential menaces. Hence
the more distant the frontiers, the more secure is Rome.
The crushing, subjugating, and pacification of foreign territory is self-evident justification. Success alone guarantees the
virtue of commanders like Pompey and Caesar.

The following selection is from Cicero, *De Provinciis Consularibus*, Secs. XI–XIV, trans. R. Gardner in *Cicero, Pro Caelio,
De Provinciis Consularibus, Pro Balbo* (Cambridge, Mass: Harvard University Press, 1965), 571–81. Reprinted by permission of
the publishers and *The Loeb Classical Library*.

In regard to this, during my consulship and on my proposal, a thanksgiving for ten days was for the first time voted to
Gnaeus Pompeius after Mithridates had been slain and the Mith-
ridatic War concluded. It was again on my proposal that a thanksgiving awarded to those of consular rank was for the first time
doubled in length, for you sided with me, after dispatches from
the same Pompeius had been read out, announcing the termina-
tion of all wars by land and sea, and awarded to him a thanksgiving for ten days. On this recent occasion, therefore, I admired the
strength of mind and magnanimity of Gnaeus Pompeius because,
while he had been himself preferred to distinctions beyond all
other men, he was for granting greater distinction to another than
he himself had obtained. So then, about that public thanksgiving
for which I voted, the thanksgiving itself was something duly offered to the Immortal Gods, the customs of our ancestors, and the
advantage of the State, but the dignified language, the unexampled distinction, and the number of days were concessions to the
merit and glory of Caesar himself. We have lately had referred to us
the question of pay for his troops. Not only did I vote for it, but I
also did my utmost to make you do the same; I answered at length

those who disagreed, I was one of those who were present to draft the resolution of the Senate. Then also I thought more of the man than of any kind of necessity. For I believed, that even without this help in money, he could maintain his army with the booty which he had previously won, and finish the war; but I certainly did not think that the lustre and glory of his triumph ought to be lessened by meanness on our part. A resolution was passed concerning ten legates. Some absolutely refused to approve them, others wanted precedents, others were for putting off the matter, and others were in favour of granting them without any complimentary expressions. On this matter also I spoke in such terms that every one could understand that I did what I felt was for the interest of the State with greater generosity owing to the merits of Caesar himself.

XII. Now, however, when it is a question of assigning provinces, whereas I was allowed to discuss all those matters in silence, I find myself interrupted. Although these former proposals concerned honours to be conferred on Caesar nothing else now moves me except military considerations and the supreme interest of the State. For what reason is there why Caesar should himself wish to linger in his province, save that he should hand over to the State fully accomplished a work on which he is engaged? I suppose it is the pleasantness of the country, the beauty of the cities, the culture and refinement of the inhabitants and peoples, the desire for victory, the extension of the boundaries of our Empire, that detain him! What can be found more savage than those lands, more uncivilized than those towns, more ferocious than those peoples, what moreover more admirable than all those victories, what more distant than the Ocean? Will his return to his country be in any way unwelcome either to the People who sent him out, or to the Senate who honoured him? Does the passing of time whet our longing for him, or make us forget his existence more and more, and do those laurels won at the cost of great dangers lose their freshness after so long a time? And so, if there are some who do not love the man, there is no reason why they should recall him from his province; for that means to recall him to glory, to a triumph, to congratulations, to the highest honours the Senate can bestow, to the favour of the Equestrian Order, to the affection of the People. But if he is in no hurry to enjoy such brilliant fortune, simply for the advantage of the State, so that he may finish all the work he has begun, what ought I, a senator, to do, who, even if he wished otherwise, should be bound to consult the interests of the State?

But as for myself, Conscript Fathers, I feel that to-day our assignment of the provinces should aim at the maintenance of a lasting peace. For who does not see that in all other quarters we are free from any danger and even from any suspicion of war? We have long seen how those vast seas, whose unrest endangered not only voyages but even cities and military roads, have become, thanks to the valour of Gnaeus Pompeius, from the Ocean to the farthest shores of Pontus, as it were one safe and closed harbour in the control of the Roman People; how, thanks also to Pompeius, of those peoples whose surging multitudes could sweep over our provinces, some have been cut off, others driven back; and how Asia, once the frontier of our power, is now itself bounded by three new provinces. I can speak of every region of the world, of every kind of enemies. There is no race which has not either been so utterly destroyed that it hardly exists, or so thoroughly subdued that it remains submissive, or so pacified that it rejoices in our victory and rule.

XIII. Under Gaius Caesar's command, Conscript Fathers, we have fought a war in Gaul; before we merely repelled attacks. Our commanders always thought that those peoples ought to be beaten back in war rather than attacked. The great Gaius Marius himself, whose divine and outstanding bravery was our stay after grievous disasters and losses suffered by the Roman People, drove back vast hordes of Gauls that were streaming into Italy, but did not himself penetrate to their cities and dwelling-places. Just recently that gallant man, who was associated with me in my labours, my dangers, and my counsels, I mean Gaius Pomptinus, broke up by his battles a war that was begun on a sudden by the Allobroges and fomented by this wicked Conspiracy, subdued those who had attacked us, and content with that victory, after the country had been freed from alarm, rested on his laurels. Gaius Caesar's plans, I observe, have been far different. For he did not think that he ought to fight only against those whom he saw already in arms against the Roman People, but that the whole of Gaul should be brought under our sway. And so he has, with brilliant success, crushed in battle the fiercest and greatest tribes of Germania and Helvetia; the rest he has terrified, checked and subdued, and taught them to submit to the rule of the Roman People. Over these regions and races, which no writings, no spoken word, no report had before made known to us, over them have our general, our soldiers, and the arms of the Roman People made their way. A mere path, Conscript Fathers, was the only part of Gaul that we held before; the rest was peopled by tribes who were either enemies of our rule or rebels against it, or by men unknown to us or known only as wild, savage and warlike—tribes which no one who ever lived would not wish to see crushed and subdued. From the very beginning of our Empire we have had no wise statesman who did not regard Gaul as the greatest danger to our Empire. But, owing to the might and numbers of those peoples, never before have we engaged in conflict with them as a whole. We have always withstood them whenever we have been challenged. Now at length we have reached the consummation that the limits of our Empire and of those lands are one and the same.

XIV. The Alps, not without the favour of heaven, were once raised high by nature as a rampart to Italy. For if that approach to our country had lain open to savage hordes of Gauls, never would this city have provided a home and chosen seat for sovereign rule. Let the Alps now sink in the earth! For there is nothing beyond those mountain peaks as far as the Ocean, of which Italy need stand in dread. Yet one or two summers, and fear or hope, punishment or rewards, arms or laws can bind the whole of Gaul to us with eternal fetters. But if we leave this work not rounded-off and in the rough, the power of Gaul, cut back though it may have been, will some day revive and burst forth anew into war.

Cato: On the Rhodian War

Voices of dissent were few and largely unheard. Little is preserved now of the internal opposition to Roman imperialism in the age of expansion. Such opposition would not suit the image perpetuated by subsequent literature and hence has almost dropped out of the tradition. Marcus Porcius Cato the Elder (234–149 B.C.) was the virtual embodiment of old Roman virtues: the sturdy farmer, staunchly opposed to the infiltration of Hellenic ideas and principles. He is often regarded as an isolationist in foreign policy. That picture needs a corrective. Cato did not advocate the contraction of frontiers, but simply the avoidance of unnecessary entanglements and antagonisms which would sap Rome's resources and diminish her moral standing. Similarly, his anti-intellectualism was something of a pose. Cato was himself a learned man in both Greek and Latin letters. He was an eloquent and forceful orator, an influential historian, and an author. Unhappily, only a lengthy tract on Italian agriculture has been preserved in its entirety. The dissenting speeches on foreign policy do not survive. But the fragments of one imporant oration warrant reproduction. In 167 B.C., after a bitter war, Rome had crushed the resurgent power of Macedon and ended forever the Macedonian monarchy. Not all the states of the east were pleased with that victory. Even Rome's most consistent ally, the island of Rhodes, had attempted to intervene and negotiate a peace before the conflict was over, evidently fearing a collapse of the balance of power. Once the war was over, many Roman leaders were furious at the Rhodian action and sought to retaliate upon their ally. Cato spoke up in opposition, pointing to the reckless arrogance which seeks to punish friend and foe alike. In compelling language he warned of the abandonment of ancient principles, the dangers to Rome's international prestige, and the unwelcome effects of imperialism upon Roman character. Only a few lines remain of the speech but they are worthy of preservation.

The following selection is from Aulus Gellius, *Attic Nights*, Book VI, Sec. 3 (with omissions), trans. John C. Rolfe in *The Attic Nights of Aulus Gellius*, II (Cambridge, Mass.: Harvard University Press, 1927), 15, 17, 21, 25, 29, 31. Reprinted by permission of the publishers and *The Loeb Classical Library*.

I am aware that in happy, successful and prosperous times the minds of most men are wont to be puffed up, and their arrogance and self-confidence to wax and swell. Therefore I am now gravely concerned, since this enterprise has gone on so successfully, lest something adverse may happen in our deliberations, to bring to naught our good fortune, and lest this joy of ours may become too extravagant. Adversity subdues and shows what ought to be done; prosperity, since it inspires joy, commonly turns men aside from wise counsel and right understanding. Therefore it is with the greater emphasis that I advise and urge that this matter be put off for a few days, until we regain our self-command after so great rejoicing.

＊   ＊   ＊

And I really think that the Rhodians did not wish us to end the war as we did, with a victory over king Perses. But it was not the Rhodians alone who had that feeling, but I believe that many peoples and many nations agreed with them. And I am inclined to think that some of them did not wish us success, not in order that we might be disgraced, but because they feared that if there were no one of whom we stood in dread, we would do whatsoever we chose. I think, then, that it was with an eye to their own free- dom that they held that opinion, in order not to be under our sole dominion and enslaved to us. But for all that, the Rhodians never publicly aided Perses. Reflect how much more cautiously we deal with one another as individuals. For each one of us, if he thinks that anything is being done contrary to his interests, strives with might and main to prevent it; but they in spite of all permitted this very thing to happen.

＊   ＊   ＊

Shall we, then, of a sudden abandon these great services given and received and this strong friendship? Shall we be the first to do what we say they merely wished to do?

＊   ＊   ＊

He who uses the strongest language against them says that they wished to be our enemies. Pray is there any one of you who, so far as he is concerned, would think it fair to suffer punishment because he is accused of having wished to do wrong? No one, I think; for so far as I am concerned, I should not. . . . "What? Is there any law so severe as to provide that if anyone wish to do so and so, he be fined a thousand sesterces, provided that be less than half his property; if anyone shall desire to have more than five hun- dred acres, let the fine be so much; if anyone shall wish to have a greater number of cattle, let the fine be thus and so. In fact, we all wish to have more, and we do so with impunity. . . . But if it is not right for honour to be conferred because anyone says that he wished to do well, but yet did not do so, shall the Rhodians suffer, not because they did wrong, but because they are said to have wished to do wrong?

* * *

They say that the Rhodians are arrogant, bringing a charge against them which I should on no account wish to have brought against me and my children. Suppose they are arrogant. What is that to us? Are you to be angry merely because someone is more arrogant than we are?

Sallust: *Letter of Mithridates*

Cicero might sing paeans to Roman conquerors of Asia and Gaul. But a younger contemporary of Cicero, Gaius Sallustius Crispus (86–34 B.C.), pointed to the other side of the coin. Sallust was himself a politician, caught up in the intrigues and maneuvers that marked late Republican Rome. Indeed, he was an adherent and admirer of Julius Caesar. But disillusionment came later in life. Sallust abandoned the active for the contemplative life. He turned his hand to the writing of history, utilizing the opportunity to propagate gloomy reflections upon the course of Republican Rome. Among other items, the results of Roman overseas expansion received Sallust's strictures. It was easy to praise the victor; but who was to speak for the victim? For the foreign opponent the march of Roman arms did not usually mean salvation and security. There was bitter resentment in the east, played upon by Mithridates of Pontus, who was a formidable foe of Rome for three decades. Cicero had lauded Pompey's victories over Mithridates. Sallust recognized the ill-will and hostility they created. In 69 B.C. Mithridates and his ally Tigranes of Armenia sought assistance in their campaigns from Arsaces, the king of Parthia. The letter of Mithridates which appears in Sallust's *Histories* is the historian's own creation. But it reflects characteristic anti-Roman feeling in Asia. The summary of previous Roman conquests is presented in a very different light from that provided by Ennius or Polybius. The ruthlessness and greed of the conqueror who crushes friends and allies in the course of triumph here receive graphic treatment.

The following selection is from Sallust, *Histories*, Book IV, Sec. 69; trans. John C. Rolfe in *Sallust* (Cambridge, Mass.: Harvard University Press, 1955), 433–41. Reprinted by permission of the publishers and *The Loeb Classical Library*.

King Mithridates to King Arsaces, Greeting. All those who in the time of their prosperity are asked to form an offensive alliance ought to consider, first, whether it is possible for them to keep peace at that time; and secondly, whether what is asked of them is wholly right and safe, honourable or dishonourable. If it were possible for you to enjoy lasting peace, if no treacherous foes were near your borders, if to crush the Roman power would not bring you glorious fame, I should not venture to sue for your alliance, and it would be vain for me to hope to unite my misfortunes with your prosperity. But the considerations which might seem to give you pause, such as the anger against Tigranes inspired in you by the recent war, and my lack of success, if you but consent to regard them in the right light, will be special incentives. For Tigranes is at your mercy and will accept an alliance on any terms which you may desire, while so far as I am concerned, although Fortune has deprived me of much, she has bestowed upon me the experience necessary for giving good advice; and since I am no longer at the height of my power, I shall serve as an example of how you may conduct your own affairs with more prudence, a lesson highly advantageous to the prosperous.

In fact, the Romans have one inveterate motive for making war upon all nations, peoples and kings; namely, a deep-seated desire for dominion and for riches. Therefore they first began a war with Philip, king of Macedonia, having pretended to be his friends as long as they were hard pressed by the Carthaginians. When Antiochus came to his aid, they craftily diverted him from his purpose by the surrender of Asia, and then, after Philip's power had been broken, Antiochus was robbed of all the territory this side Taurus, and of ten thousand talents. Next Perses, the son of Philip, after many battles with varying results, was formally taken under their protection before the gods of Samothrace; and then those masters of craft and artists in treachery caused his death from want of sleep, since they had made a compact not to kill him. Eumenes, whose friendship they boastfully parade, they first betrayed to Antiochus as the price of peace; later, having made him the guardian of a captured territory, they transformed him by means of imposts and insults from a king into the most wretched of slaves. Then, having forged an unnatural will, they led his son Aristonicus in triumph like an enemy, because he had tried to recover his father's realm. They took possession of Asia, and finally, on the death of Nicomedes, they seized upon all Bithynia, although Nysa, whom Nicomedes had called queen, unquestionably had a son.

Why should I mention my own case? Although I was separated from their empire on every side by kingdoms and tetrarchies, yet because it was reported that I was rich and that I would not be a slave, they provoked me to war through Nicomedes. And I was not unaware of their design, but I had previously given warning of what afterwards happened, both to the Cretans, who alone retained their freedom at that time, and to king Ptolemy. But I took vengeance for the wrongs inflicted upon me; I drove Nicomedes from Bithynia, recovered Asia, the spoil taken from king Antiochus, and delivered Greece from cruel servitude. Further progress was frustrated by Archelaus, basest of slaves, who betrayed my army; and those whom cowardice or misplaced cunning kept from taking up arms, since they hoped to find safety in my misfortunes, are suffering most cruel punishment. For Ptolemy is averting hostilities from day to day by the payment of money, while the Cretans have already been attacked once and will find no respite from war until they are destroyed. As for me, I soon learned that the peace afforded by civil dissensions at Rome was really only a postponement of the struggle, and although Tigranes refused to join with me (he now admits the truth of my prediction when it is too late), though you were far away, and all the rest had submitted, I nevertheless renewed the war and routed Marcus Cotta, the Roman general, on land at Chalcedon, while on the sea I stripped him of a fine fleet. During the delay caused by my siege of Cyzicus with a great army provisions failed me, since no one in the neighbourhood rendered me aid and at the same time winter kept me off the sea. When I, therefore, without compulsion from the enemy, attempted to return into my kingdom, I lost the best of my soldiers and my fleets by shipwrecks at Parium and at Heraclea. Then when I had raised a new army at Cabira and engaged with Lucullus with varying success, scarcity once more attacked us both. He had at his command the kingdom of Ariobarzanes, unravaged by war, while I, since all the country about me had been devastated, withdrew into Armenia. Thereupon the Romans followed me, or rather followed their custom of overthrowing all monarchies, and because they were able to keep from action a huge force hemmed in by narrow defiles, boasted of the results of Tigranes' imprudence as if they had won a victory.

I pray you, then, to consider whether you believe that when we have been crushed you will be better able to resist the Romans, or that there will be an end to the war. I know well that you have great numbers of men and large amounts of arms and gold, and it is for that reason that I seek your alliance and the Romans your spoils. Yet my advice is, while the kingdom of Tigranes is entire, and while I still have soldiers who have been trained in warfare with the Romans, to finish far from your homes and with little labour, at the expense of our bodies, a war in which we cannot conquer or be conquered without danger to you. Do you not know that the Romans turned their arms in this direction only after Ocean had blocked their westward progress? That they have possessed nothing since the beginning of their existence except what they have stolen: their home, their wives, their lands, their empire? Once vagabonds without fatherland, without parents, created to be the scourge of the whole world, no laws, human or divine, prevent them from seizing and destroying allies and friends, those near them and those afar off, weak or powerful, and from considering every government which does not serve them, especially monarchies, as their enemies.

Of a truth, few men desire freedom, the greater part are content with just masters; we are suspected of being rivals of the Romans and future avengers. But you, who possess Seleucea, greatest of cities, and the realm of Perses famed for its riches, what can you expect from them other than guile in the present and war in the future? The Romans have weapons against all men, the sharpest where victory yields the greatest spoils; it is by audacity, by deceit, and by joining war to war that they have grown great. Following their usual custom, they will destroy everything or perish in the

attempt . . . and this is not difficult if you on the side of Mesopo-
tamia and we on that of Armenia surround their army, which is
without supplies and without allies, and has been saved so far only
by its good fortune or by our own errors. You will gain the glory
of having rendered aid to great kings and of having crushed the
plunderers of all the nations. This is my advice and this course I
urge you to follow; do not prefer by our ruin to put off your own
for a time rather than by our alliance to conquer.

Part Two

THE REPUBLICAN
CONSTITUTION

The Roman constitution was no written document. It was the product of many generations of evolution, often accompanied by internal strife and struggle. Rome emerges into recorded history under monarchical rule and as the creation of outside powers and immigrants. Like many other ancient states, the Roman monarchy yielded eventually to an aristocratic cabal, always depicted in retrospect as "liberation." The birth of the Republic meant the exercise of authority by a tight group of oligarchic families who controlled all secular and religious institutions and who imposed or perpetuated a rigid caste system. The progress of time produced greater sophistication among the "plebeians," the emergence of their own leaders, and the gradual opening of institutions to wide participation.

Self-consciousness about constitutional development, as always, emerges at a late stage. When the theorizing began it was imported from abroad. Polybius' admiration for Rome's achievement led him to an examination of the institutions on which it was founded. But his political theory operated within fixed categories set by a long tradition of Greek speculation. Plato and Aristotle had dissected constitutional forms in the abstract and found a rotation of monarchy, aristocracy, and democracy. Each of the forms had its advantages, each had a tendency to slip into its own corruption: monarchy into tyranny, aristocracy into oligarchy, democracy into mob rule. If stability were to be had, government required a balanced combination of all three elements. That was the tradition in which Polybius wrote. The Roman constitution produced a workable machinery whose success outstripped all predecessors. Consequently, Polybius fitted it into the ideal structure constructed by Greek theory; it was a "mixed constitution" which combined absolute authority in the field, aristocratic management at home, and widespread participation and acquiescence by the "people."

Polybius' schematic construction was attractive and flattering. Naturally it appealed also to Roman thinkers. When Cicero retired to speculate about the Roman constitution he saw it through Polybius' eyes and adopted Polybius' scheme. The balanced harmony of classes and institutions was the way in which most Romans preferred to think of their governmental structure. But Sallust, as one might expect, was not persuaded. The attractive design may have once existed; in his own day, however, Sallust had witnessed the crumbling of institutions. He felt the necessity to penetrate beyond structural analysis. Not that Sallust's moralizing approach provided sounder methodology. But he detected a profound change in the practices, attitudes, and aims of a people who had abandoned the traditions of their ancestors. The two views provide a healthy contrast and a revealing guide to the thinking of the late Republic on the Roman constitution.

Cicero: On the State

It would be foolish to attempt a summary of Cicero's career and contributions within the short compass of a paragraph. A busy and full life on the public stage would have left most men with little time for literary productivity. But Cicero was no ordinary mind. He played an active and prominent part in Roman politics. At the same time, his intellectual contributions are staggering in both bulk and quality. Cicero's speeches lifted Roman oratory to a level unsurpassed before or since; his writings on rhetoric and rhetorical theory were models for later generations; his voluminous correspondence supplies much of the most precious information on his entire age; he was an acknowledged and imitated master of Latin prose. Not the least of Cicero's accomplishments were his works on philosophy and political theory. In these areas he was no innovator. But his translations and reworking of Greek philosophical tracts opened them to a wider audience and exercised a potent impact upon succeeding generations. It is testimony to Cicero's style and influence that his works survived while those of most of his Greek predecessors have perished. Political theory was close to Cicero's heart. He witnessed the stresses and pressures brought to bear on the Roman constitution of his own day. Cicero's treatise on the constitution is couched in the form of a dialogue set in the previous generation, when it could be analyzed in its purer form. The *De Republica* (*On the State*) follows Plato and Polybius: the ideal form of government combines the best qualities of monarchy, aristocracy, and democracy. For Cicero, that form is best exemplified by Rome's own experience. Scipio Aemilianus, Cicero's spokesman in his dialogue, records the growth of Roman institutions as the model for the best obtainable governmental form. The Roman constitution was not the creature of one man's imagination, but the product of time and the collective wisdom of statesmen.

The following selection is from Cicero, *De Republica*, Book I, Secs. 25–35, 42–46; Book II, Sec. 1; trans. C. W. Keyes in *Cicero, De Republica, De Legibus* (Cambridge, Mass.: Harvard University Press, 1959), 65–83, 97–107, 111–13. Reprinted by permission of the publishers and *The Loeb Classical Library*.

XXV. Scipio: Well, then, a commonwealth is the property of a people. But a people is not any collection of human beings brought together in any sort of way, but an assemblage of people in large numbers associated in an agreement with respect to justice and a partnership for the common good. The first cause of such an association is not so much the weakness of the individual as a certain social spirit which nature has implanted in man. For man is not a solitary or unsocial creature, but born with such a nature that not even under conditions of great prosperity of every sort [is he willing to be isolated from his fellow men.] . . .

. . . In a short time a scattered and wandering multitude had become a body of citizens by mutual agreement. . . .

XXVI. . . . certain seeds, as we may call them, for [otherwise] no source for the other virtues nor for the State itself could be discovered. Such an assemblage of men, therefore, originating for the reason I have

mentioned, established itself in a definite place, at first in order to provide dwellings; and this place being fortified by its natural situation
and by their labours, they called such a collection of dwellings a town
or city, and provided it with shrines and gathering places which were
common property. Therefore every people, which is such a gathering
of large numbers as I have described, every city, which is an orderly settlement of a people, every commonwealth, which, as I said, is "the
property of a people," must be governed by some deliberative body if
it is to be permanent. And this deliberative body must, in the first place,
always owe its beginning to the same cause as that which produced the
State itself. In the second place, this function must either be granted to
one man, or to certain selected citizens, or must be assumed by the whole
body of citizens. And so when the supreme authority is in the hands of
one man, we call him a king, and the form of this State a kingship.
When selected citizens hold this power, we say that the State is ruled by
an aristocracy. But a popular government (for so it is called) exists
when all the power is in the hands of the people. And any one of these
three forms of government (if only the bond which originally joined the
citizens together in the partnership of the State holds fast), though not
perfect or in my opinion the best, is tolerable, though one of them may be
superior to another. For either a just and wise king, or a select number
of leading citizens, or even the people itself, though this is the least
commendable type, can nevertheless, as it seems, form a government that
is not unstable, provided that no elements of injustice or greed are mingled with it.

XXVII. But in kingships the subjects have too small a share in the
administration of justice and in deliberation; and in aristocracies the
masses can hardly have their share of liberty, since they are entirely excluded from deliberation for the common weal and from power; and
when all the power is in the people's hands, even though they exercise
it with justice and moderation, yet the resulting equality itself is inequitable, since it allows no distinctions in rank. Therefore, even though the
Persian Cyrus was the most just and wisest of kings, that form of government does not seem to me the most desirable, since "the property of
the people" (for that is what a commonwealth is, as I have said) is ad-
ministered at the nod and caprice of one man; even though the Mas-
silians, now under our protection, are ruled with the greatest justice by
a select number of their leading citizens, such a situation is nevertheless
to some extent like slavery for a people; and even though the Athenians
at certain periods, after they had deprived the Areopagus of its power,
succeeded in carrying on all their public business by the resolutions and
decrees of the people, their State, because it had no definite distinctions
in rank, could not maintain its fair renown.

XXVIII. I am now speaking of these three forms of government, not when they are confused and mingled with one another, but when they retain their appropriate character. All of them are, in the first place, subject each to the faults I have mentioned, and they suffer from other dangerous faults in addition: for before every one of them lies a slippery and precipitous path leading to a certain depraved form that is a close neighbour to it. For underneath the tolerable, or, if you like, the lovable King Cyrus (to cite him as a pre-eminent example) lies the utterly cruel Phalaris, impelling him to an arbitrary change of character; for the absolute rule of one man will easily and quickly degenerate into a tyranny like his. And a close neighbour to the excellent Massilian government, conducted by a few leading citizens, is such a partisan combination of thirty men as once ruled Athens. And as for the absolute power of the Athenian people—not to seek other examples of popular government—when it changed into the fury and licence of a mob . . .

XXIX. . . . and likewise some other form usually rises from those I have mentioned, and remarkable indeed are the periodical revolutions and circular courses followed by the constant changes and sequences in governmental forms. A wise man should be acquainted with these changes, but it calls for great citizens and for a man of almost divine powers to foresee them when they threaten, and, while holding the reins of government, to direct their courses and keep them under his control. Therefore I consider a fourth form of government the most commendable—that form which is a well-regulated mixture of the three which I mentioned at first.

XXX. LAELIUS: I know that is your opinion, Africanus, for I have often heard you say so. Nevertheless, if it will not give you too much trouble, I should like to know which you consider the best of the three forms of government of which you have been speaking. For it might help us somewhat to understand . . .

XXXI. SCIPIO: . . . and every State is such as its ruler's character and will make it. Hence liberty has no dwelling-place in any State except that in which the people's power is the greatest, and surely nothing can be sweeter than liberty; but if it is not the same for all, it does not deserve the name of liberty. And how can it be the same for all, I will not say in a kingdom, where there is no obscurity or doubt about the slavery of the subject, but even in States where everyone is ostensibly free? I mean States in which the people vote, elect commanders and officials, are canvassed for their votes, and have bills proposed to them, but really grant only what they would have to grant even if they were unwilling to do so, and are asked to give to others what they do not possess themselves. For they have no share in the governing power, in the deliberative function, or in the courts, over which selected judges preside, for those privileges are granted on the basis of birth or wealth. But in a free nation, such as the Rhodians or the Athenians, there is not one of the citizens who [may not hold the offices of State and take an active part in the government.] . . .

XXXII. [Our authorities] say [that] when one person or a few stand out from the crowd as richer and more prosperous, then, as a result of the haughty and arrogant behaviour of these, there arises [a government of one or a few], the cowardly and weak giving way and bowing down to the pride of wealth. But if the people would maintain their rights, they say that no form of government would be superior, either in liberty or happiness, for they themselves would be masters of the laws and the courts, of war and peace, of international agreements, and of every citizen's life and property; this government alone, they believe, can rightly be called a commonwealth, that is, "the property of the people." And it is for that reason, they say, that "the property of the people" is often liberated from the domination of kings or senators, while free peoples do not seek kings or the power and wealth of aristocracies. And indeed they claim that this free popular government ought not to be entirely rejected on account of the excesses of an unbridled mob, for, according to them, when a sovereign people is pervaded by a spirit of harmony and tests every measure by the standard of their own safety and liberty, no form of government is less subject to change or more stable. And they insist that harmony is very easily obtainable in a State where the interests of all are the same, for discord arises from conflicting interests, where different measures are advantageous to different citizens. Therefore they maintain that when a senate has been supreme, the State has never had a stable government, and that such stability is less attainable by far in kingdoms, in which, as Ennius says,

No sacred partnership or honour is.

Therefore, since law is the bond which unites the civic association, and the justice enforced by law is the same for all, by what justice can an association of citizens be held together when there is no equality among the citizens? For if we cannot agree to equalize men's wealth, and equality of innate ability is impossible, the legal rights at least of those who are citizens of the same commonwealth ought to be equal. For what is a State except an association or partnership in justice? . . .

XXXIII. . . . Indeed they think that States of the other kinds have no right at all to the names which they arrogate to themselves. For why should I give the name of king, the title of Jupiter the Best, to a man who is greedy for personal power and absolute authority, a man who lords it over an oppressed people? Should I not rather call him tyrant? For tyrants may be merciful as well as oppressive; so that the only difference between the nations governed by these rulers is that between the slaves of a kind and those of a cruel master; for in any case the subjects must be slaves. And how could Sparta, at the time when the mode of life inculcated by her constitution was considered so excellent, be assured of always having good and just kings, when a person of any sort, if he was born of the royal family, had to be accepted as king? As to aristocrats, who could tolerate men that have claimed the title without the people's acquiescence, but merely by their own will? For how is a man adjudged to be "the best"? On the basis of knowledge, skill, learning, [and similar qualities surely, not because of his own desire to possess the title!] . . .

XXXIV. . . . . If [the State] leaves [the selection of its rulers] to chance, it will be as quickly overturned as a ship whose pilot should be chosen by lot from among the passengers. But if a free people chooses the men to whom it is to entrust its fortunes, and, since it desires its own safety, chooses the best men, then certainly the safety of the State depends upon the wisdom of its best men, especially since Nature has provided not only that those men who are superior in virtue and in spirit should rule the weaker, but also that the weaker should be willing to obey the stronger.

But they claim that this ideal form of State has been rejected on account of the false notions of men, who, through their ignorance of virtue —for just as virtue is possessed by only a few, so it can be distinguished and perceived by only a few—think that the best men are those who are rich, prosperous, or born of famous families. For when, on account of this mistaken notion of the common people, the State begins to be ruled by the riches, instead of the virtue, of a few men, these rulers tenaciously retain the title, though they do not possess the character, of the "best." For riches, names, and power, when they lack wisdom and the knowledge of how to live and to rule over others, are full of dishonour and insolent pride, nor is there any more depraved type of State than that in which the richest are accounted the best. But what can be nobler than the government of the State by virtue? For then the man who rules others is not himself a slave to any passion, but has already acquired for himself all those qualities to which he is training and summoning his fellows. Such a man imposes no laws upon the people that he does not obey himself, but puts his own life before his fellow-citizens as their law. If a single individual of this character could order all things properly in a State, there would be no need of more than one ruler; or if the citizens as a body could see what was best and agree upon it, no one would desire a selected group of rulers. It has been the difficulty of formulating policies that has transferred the power from a king to a larger number; and the perversity and rashness of popular assemblies that have transferred it from the many to the few. Thus, between the weakness of a single ruler and the rashness of the many, aristocracies have occupied that intermediate position which represents the utmost moderation; and in a State ruled by its best men, the citizens must necessarily enjoy the greatest happiness, being freed from all cares and worries, when once they have entrusted the preservation of their tranquillity to others, whose duty it is to guard it vigilantly and never to allow the people to think that their interests are being neglected by their rulers. For that equality of legal rights of which free peoples are so fond cannot be maintained (for the people themselves, though free and unrestrained, give very many special powers to many individuals, and create great distinctions among men and the honours granted to them), and what is called equality is really most inequitable. For when equal honour is given to the highest and the lowest—for men of both types must exist in every nation—then this very "fairness" is most unfair; but this cannot happen in States ruled by their best citizens. These arguments and others like them, Laelius, are approximately those which are advanced by men who consider this form of government the best.

XXXV. LAELIUS: But what about yourself, Scipio? Which of these three forms do you consider the best?

SCIPIO: You are right to ask which I consider the best of the three, for I do not approve of any of them when employed by itself, and consider the form which is a combination of all of them superior to any single one of them. But if I were compelled to approve one single unmixed form, [I might choose] the kingship . . . the name of king seems like that of father to us, since the king provides for the citizens as if they were his own children, and is more eager to protect them than . . . to be sustained by the care of one man who is the most virtuous and most eminent. But here are the aristocrats, with the claim that they can do this more effectively, and that there will be more wisdom in the counsels of several than in those of one man, and an equal amount of fairness and scrupulousness. And here also are the people, shouting with a loud voice that they are willing to obey neither one nor a few, that nothing is sweeter than liberty even to wild beasts, and that all who are slaves, whether to a king or to an aristocracy, are deprived of liberty. Thus kings attract us by our affection for them, aristocracies by their wisdom, and popular governments by their freedom, so that in comparing them it is difficult to say which one prefers.

*   *   *

XLII. When I have set forth my ideas in regard to the form of State which I consider the best, I shall have to take up in greater detail those changes to which States are liable, though I think it will not be at all easy for any such changes to take place in the State which I have in mind. But the first and most certain of these changes is the one that takes place in kingships: when the king begins to be unjust, that form of government is immediately at an end, and the king has become a tyrant.

This is the worst sort of government, though closely related to the best. If the best men overthrow it, as usually happens, then the State is in the second of its three stages; for this form is similar to a kingship, being one in which a paternal council of leading men makes good provision for the people's welfare. But if the people themselves have killed or driven out the tyrant, they govern rather moderately, as long as they are wise and prudent, and, delighting in their exploit, they endeavour to maintain the government they have themselves set up. But if the people ever rebel against a just king and deprive him of his kingdom, or, as happens more frequently, taste the blood of the aristocracy and subject the whole State to their own caprices (and do not dream, Laelius, that any sea or any conflagration is so powerful that it cannot be more easily subdued than an unbridled multitude enjoying unwonted power), then we have a condition which is splendidly described by Plato, if only I can reproduce his description in Latin; it is difficult, but I will attempt it. XLIII. He says: "When the insatiable throats of the people have become dry with the thirst for liberty, and, served by evil ministers, they have drained in their thirst a draught of liberty which, instead of being moderately tempered, is too strong for them, then, unless the magistrates and men of high rank are very mild and indulgent, serving them with liberty in generous quantities, the people persecute them, charge them with crime and impeach them, calling them despots, kings, and tyrants." I think you are acquainted with this passage.

LAELIUS: It is very familiar to me.

SCIPIO: He continues thus: "Those who follow the lead of prominent citizens are persecuted by such a people and called willing slaves; but those who, though in office, try to act like private citizens, and those private citizens who try to destroy all distinction between a private citizen and a magistrate are praised to the skies and loaded with honours. It necessarily follows in such a State that liberty prevails everywhere, to such an extent that not only are homes one and all without a master, but the vice of anarchy extends even to the domestic animals, until finally the father fears his son, the son flouts his father, all sense of shame disappears, and all is so absolutely free that there is no distinction between citizen and alien; the schoolmaster fears and flatters his pupils, and pupils despise their masters; youths take on the gravity of age, and old men stoop to the games of youth, for fear they may be disliked by their juniors and seem to them too serious. Under such conditions even the slaves come to behave with unseemly freedom, wives have the same rights as their husbands, and in the abundance of liberty even the dogs, the horses, and the asses are so free in their running about that men must make way for them in the streets. Therefore," he concludes, "the final result of this boundless licence is that the minds of the citizens become so squeamish and sensitive that, if the authority of government is exercised in the smallest degree, they become angry and cannot bear it. On this account they begin to neglect the laws as well, and so finally are utterly without a master of any kind."

XLIV. LAELIUS: You have given us his description with great exactness.

SCIPIO: Well, to return now to my own style of discourse, he also says that from this exaggerated licence, which is the only thing such people call liberty, tyrants spring up as from a root, and are, as it were, engendered. For just as an excess of power in the hands of the aristocrats results in the overthrow of an aristocracy, so liberty itself reduces a people who possess it in too great degree to servitude. Thus everything which is in excess—when, for instance, either in the weather, or in the fields, or in men's bodies, conditions have been too favourable—is usually changed into its opposite; and this is especially true in States, where such excess of liberty either in nations or in individuals turns into an excess of servitude. This extreme liberty gives birth to a tyrant and the utterly unjust and cruel servitude of the tyranny. For out of such an ungoverned, or rather, untamed, populace someone is usually chosen as leader against those leading citizens who have already been subjected to persecution and cast down from their leadership—some bold and depraved man, who shamelessly harasses oftentimes even those who have deserved well of the State, and curries favour with the people by bestowing upon them the property of others as well as his own. To such a man, because he has much reason to be afraid if he remains a private citizen, official power is given and continually renewed; he is also surrounded by armed guards, as was Pisistratus at Athens; and finally he emerges as a tyrant over the very people who have raised him to power. If the better citizens overthrow such a tyrant, as often happens, then the State is re-established; but if it is the bolder sort who do so, then we have that oligarchy which is only a tyranny of another kind. This same form of government also arises from the excellent rule of an aristocracy, when some bad influence turns the leading citizens themselves from the right path. Thus the ruling power of the State, like a ball, is snatched from kings by tyrants, from tyrants by aristocrats or the people, and from them again by an oligarchical faction or a tyrant, so that no single form of government ever maintains itself very long.

XLV. Since this is true, the kingship, in my opinion, is by far the best of the three primary forms, but a moderate and balanced form of government which is a combination of the three good simple forms is preferable even to the kingship. For there should be a supreme and royal element in the State, some power also ought to be granted to the leading citizens, and certain matters should be left to the judgment and desires of the masses. Such a constitution, in the first place, offers in a high degree a sort of equality, which is a thing free men can hardly do without for any considerable length of time, and, secondly, it has stability. For the primary forms already mentioned degenerate easily into the corresponding perverted forms, the king being replaced by a despot, the aristocracy by an oligarchical faction, and the people by a mob and anarchy; but whereas these forms are frequently changed into new ones, this does not usually happen in the case of the mixed and evenly balanced constitution, except through great faults in the governing class. For there is no reason for a change when every citizen is firmly established in his own station, and there underlies it no perverted form into which it can plunge and sink.

XLVI. But I am afraid that you, Laelius, and you, my very dear and learned friends, may think, if I spend more time upon this aspect of the subject, that my discourse is rather that of a master or teacher than of one who is merely considering these matters in company with yourselves. Therefore I will pass to a topic which is familiar to everyone, and which we ourselves discussed some time ago. For I am convinced, I believe, and I declare that no other form of government is comparable, either in its general character, in its distribution of powers, or in the training it gives, with that which our ancestors received from their own forefathers, and have handed down to us. Therefore, if you have no objection—since you have desired to hear me discourse upon matters with which you are already familiar—I will explain the character of this constitution and show why it is the best; and, using our own government as my pattern, I will fit to it, if I can, all I have to say about the ideal State. If I can keep to this intention and carry it through, the task that Laelius has imposed upon me will, in my opinion, have been abundantly accomplished.

XLVII. LAELIUS: The task is yours indeed, Scipio, and yours alone; for who is better qualified than yourself to speak of the institutions of our ancestors, since you yourself are descended from most famous forefathers? Or who is better able to speak of the ideal State? For if we are to have such a constitution (surely at present that is not the case), who would be more prominent in its administration than yourself? Or who is better qualified to speak of provisions for the future, when you have provided for all future time by freeing our city from the two dangers that threatened it?

*　　　　*　　　　*

Cato used to say that our constitution was superior to those of other States on account of the fact that almost every one of these other commonwealths had been established by one man, the author of their laws and institutions; for example, Minos in Crete, Lycurgus in Sparta, and in Athens, whose form of government had frequently changed, first Theseus, and later Draco, Solon, Clisthenes, and many others; and last of all, when the State lay bloodless and prostrate, that learned man of Phalerum, Demetrius, revived it again. On the other hand our own commonwealth was based upon the genius, not of one man, but of many; it was founded, not in one generation, but in a long period of several centuries and many ages of men. For, said he, there never has lived a man possessed of so great genius that nothing could escape him, nor could the combined powers of all the men living at one time possibly make all necessary provisions for the future without the aid of actual experience and the test of time.

Sallust: The Conspiracy of Catiline

That it was institutions, as well as the quality of men, which made Rome great was an article of faith among Roman thinkers. Sallust was no exception. He accepted the standard notion of an heroic age in Rome's past when men were taught to restrict their ambitions to the service of the state and when a constitution founded on law bound all classes together in a common enterprise. But, for Sallust, the institutions are no better than the men who operate them. To praise the structure of government when its personnel can no longer measure up to its principles is myopia. Sallust experienced the breakdown of the Republican machinery and his explanation concentrates heavily on the moral degeneration of Roman character. Depression and anger led him to write a monograph on the conspiracy of Catiline which he witnessed as a young man. For him, Catiline's movement represented an inevitable outburst against a corrupt oligarchy and a debased system. Not that Sallust expresses sympathy for Catiline and his followers. Rather, the conspiracy itself is employed as a vehicle to criticize a rotten society which could have produced such a man and such a movement. It gives the historian an opportunity to make some general reflections. Romans had once respected their institutions. The growth of Rome's prestige and power was due to disciplined citizens whose only ambition was renown and the perpetuation of the state's interest. But unbroken success led to baser ambitions. Rome tasted luxury and acquired greed. Antique traditions lost their appeal. The collapse of external opposition turned restless Romans against one another in a frantic competition for money and power.

A new generation lacked sound models to emulate and either wallowed in idleness or competed for gain. In Sallust's view, admiration for the constitution is pure antiquarianism. The process of decline is more telling than the resurrection of a lost tradition.

The following selection is from Sallust, *Catiline*, Secs. 2-14, 36-39; trans. John C. Rolfe in *Sallust* (Cambridge, Mass.: Harvard University Press, 1955), 5-25, 63-67. Reprinted by permission of the publishers and *The Loeb Classical Library*.

Now if the mental excellence with which kings and rulers are endowed were as potent in peace as in war, human affairs would run an evener and steadier course, and you would not see power passing from hand to hand and everything in turmoil and confusion; for empire is easily retained by the qualities by which it was first won. But when sloth has usurped the place of industry, and lawlessness and insolence have superseded self-restraint and justice, the fortune of princes changes with their character. Thus the sway is always passing to the best man from the hands of his inferior.

Success in agriculture, navigation, and architecture depends invariably upon mental excellence. Yet many men, being slaves to appetite and sleep, have passed through life untaught and untrained, like mere wayfarers; in these men we see, contrary to Nature's intent, the body a source of pleasure, the soul a burden. For my own part, I consider the lives and deaths of such men as about alike, since no record is made of either. In very truth that man alone lives and makes the most of life, as it seems to me, who devotes himself to some occupation, courting the fame of a glorious deed or a noble career. But amid the wealth of opportunities Nature points out one path to one and another to another.

III. It is glorious to serve one's country by deeds; even to serve her by words is a thing not to be despised; one may become famous in peace as well as in war. Not only those who have acted, but those also who have recorded the acts of others oftentimes receive our approbation. And for myself, although I am well aware that by no means equal repute attends the narrator and the doer of deeds, yet I regard the writing of history as one of the most difficult of tasks: first, because the style and diction must be equal to the deeds recorded; and in the second place, because such criticisms as you make of others' shortcomings are thought by most men to be due to malice and envy. Furthermore, when you commemorate the distinguished merit and fame of good men, while every one is quite ready to believe you when you tell of things which he thinks he could easily do himself, everything beyond that he regards as fictitious, if not false.

When I myself was a young man, my inclinations at first led me, like many another, into public life, and there I encountered many obstacles; for instead of modesty, incorruptibility and honesty, shamelessness, bribery and rapacity held sway. And although my soul, a stranger to evil ways, recoiled from such faults, yet amid so many vices my youthful weakness was led astray and held captive by ambition; for while I took no part in the evil practices of the others, yet the desire for preferment made me the victim of the same ill-repute and jealousy as they.

IV. Accordingly, when my mind found peace after many troubles and perils and I had determined that I must pass what was left of my life aloof from public affairs, it was not my intention to waste my precious leisure in indolence and sloth, nor yet by turning to farming or the chase, to lead a life devoted to slavish employments. On the contrary, I resolved to return to a cherished purpose from which ill-starred ambition had diverted me, and write a history of the Roman people, selecting such portions as seemed to me worthy of record; and I was confirmed in this resolution by the fact that my mind was free from hope, and fear, and partisanship. I shall therefore write briefly and as truthfully as possible of the conspiracy of Catiline; for I regard that event as worthy of special notice because of the extraordinary nature of the crime and of the danger arising from it. But before beginning my narrative I must say a few words about the man's character.

V. Lucius Catilina, scion of a noble family, had great vigour both of mind and of body, but an evil and depraved nature. From youth up he revelled in civil wars, murder, pillage, and political dissension, and amid these he spent his early manhood. His body could endure hunger, cold and want of sleep to an incredible degree; his mind was reckless, cunning, treacherous, capable of any form of pretence or concealment. Covetous of others' possessions, he was prodigal of his own; he was violent in his passions. He possessed a certain amount of eloquence, but little discretion. His disordered mind ever craved the monstrous, incredible, gigantic.

After the domination of Lucius Sulla the man had been seized with a mighty desire of getting control of the government, recking little by what manner he should achieve it, provided he made himself supreme. His haughty spirit was goaded more and more every day by poverty and a sense of guilt, both of which he had augmented by the practices of which I have already spoken. He was spurred on, also, by the corruption of the public morals, which were being ruined by two great evils of an opposite character, extravagance and avarice.

Since the occasion has arisen to speak of the morals of our country, the nature of my theme seems to suggest that I go farther back and give a brief account of the institutions of our forefathers in peace and in war, how they governed the commonwealth, how great it was when they bequeathed it to us, and how by gradual changes it has ceased to be the noblest and best, and has become the worst and most vicious.

VI. The city of Rome, according to my understanding, was at the outset founded and inhabited by Trojans, who were wandering about in exile under the leadership of Aeneas and had no fixed abode; they were joined by the Aborigines, a rustic folk, without laws or government, free and unrestrained. After these two peoples, different in race, unlike in speech and mode of life, were united within the same walls, they were merged into one with incredible facility, so quickly did harmony change a heterogeneous and roving band into a commonwealth. But when this new community had grown in numbers, civilization, and territory, and was beginning to seem amply rich and amply strong, then, as is usual with mortal affairs, prosperity gave birth to envy. As a result, neighbouring kings and peoples made war upon them, and but few of their friends lent them aid; for the rest were smitten with fear and stood aloof from the danger. But the Romans, putting forth their whole energy at home and in the field, made all haste, got ready, encouraged one another, went to meet the foe, and defended their liberty, their country, and their parents by arms. Afterwards, when their prowess had averted the danger, they lent aid to their allies and friends, and established friendly relations rather by conferring than by accepting favours.

They had a constitution founded upon law, which was in name a monarchy; a chosen few, whose bodies were enfeebled by age but whose minds were fortified with wisdom, took counsel for the welfare of the state. These were called Fathers, by reason either of their age or of the similarity of their duties. Later, when the rule of the kings, which at first had tended to preserve freedom and advance the state, had degenerated into a lawless tyranny, they altered their form of government and appointed two rulers with annual power, thinking that this device would prevent men's minds from growing arrogant through unlimited authority.

VII. Now at that time every man began to lift his head higher and to have his talents more in readiness. For kings hold the good in greater suspicion than the wicked, and to them the merit of others is always fraught with danger; still the free state, once liberty was won, waxed incredibly strong and great in a remarkably short time, such was the thirst for glory that had filled men's minds. To begin with, as soon as the young men could endure the hardships of war, they were taught a soldier's duties in camp under a vigorous discipline, and they took more pleasure in handsome arms and war horses than in harlots and revelry. To such men consequently no labour was unfamiliar, no region too rough or too steep, no armed foeman was terrible; valour was all in all. Nay, their hardest struggle for glory was with one another; each man strove to be first to strike down the foe, to scale a wall, to be seen of all while doing such a deed. This they considered riches, this fair fame and high nobility. It was praise they coveted, but they were lavish of money; their aim was unbounded renown, but only such riches as could be gained honourably. I might name the battlefields on which the Romans with a mere handful of men routed great armies of their adversaries, and the cities fortified by nature which they took by assault, were it not that such a theme would carry me too far from my subject.

VIII. But beyond question Fortune holds sway everywhere. It is she that makes all events famous or obscure according to her caprice rather than in accordance with the truth. The acts of the Athenians, in my judgment, were indeed great and glorious enough, but nevertheless somewhat less important than fame represents them. But because Athens produced writers of exceptional talent, the exploits of the men of Athens are heralded throughout the world as unsurpassed. Thus the merit of those who did the deeds is rated as high as brilliant minds have been able to exalt the deeds themselves by words of praise. But the Roman people never had that advantage, since their ablest men were always most engaged with affairs; their minds were never employed apart from their bodies; the best citizen preferred action to words, and thought that his own brave deeds should be lauded by others rather than that theirs should be recounted by him.

IX. Accordingly, good morals were cultivated at home and in the field; there was the greatest harmony and little or no avarice; justice and probity prevailed among them, thanks not so much to laws as to nature. Quarrels, discords, and strife were reserved for their enemies; citizen vied with citizen only for the prize of merit. They were lavish in their offerings to the gods, frugal in the home, loyal to their friends. By practising these two qualities, boldness in warfare and justice when peace came, they watched over themselves and their country. In proof of these statements I present this convincing evidence: firstly, in time of war punishment was more often inflicted for attacking the enemy contrary to orders, or for withdrawing too tardily when recalled from the field, than for venturing to abandon the standards or to give ground under stress; and secondly, in time of peace they ruled by kindness rather than fear, and when wronged preferred forgiveness to vengeance.

X. But when our country had grown great through toil and the practice of justice, when great kings had been vanquished in war, savage tribes and mighty peoples subdued by force of arms, when Carthage, the rival of Rome's sway, had perished root and branch, and all seas and lands were open, then Fortune began to grow cruel and to bring confusion into all our affairs. Those who had found it easy to bear hardship and dangers, anxiety and adversity, found leisure and wealth, desirable under other circumstances, a burden and a curse. Hence the lust for money first, then for power, grew upon them; these were, I may say, the root of all evils. For avarice destroyed honour, integrity, and all other noble qualities; taught in their place insolence, cruelty, to neglect the gods, to set a price on everything. Ambition drove many men to become false; to have one thought locked in the breast, another ready on the tongue; to value friendships and enmities not on their merits but by the standard of self-interest, and to show a good front rather than a good heart. At first these vices grew slowly, from time to time they were punished; finally, when the disease had spread like a deadly plague, the state was changed and a government second to none in equity and excellence became cruel and intolerable.

XI. But at first men's souls were actuated less by avarice than by ambition—a fault, it is true, but not so far removed from virtue; for the noble and the base alike long for glory, honour, and power, but the former mount by the true path, whereas the latter, being destitute of noble qualities, rely upon craft and deception. Avarice implies a desire for money, which no wise man covets; steeped as it were with noxious poisons, it renders the most manly body and soul effeminate; it is ever unbounded and insatiable, nor can either plenty or want make it less. But after Lucius Sulla, having gained control of the state by arms, brought everything to a bad end from a good beginning, all men began to rob and pillage. One coveted a house, another lands; the victors showed neither moderation nor restraint, but shamefully and cruelly wronged their fellow citizens. Besides all this, Lucius Sulla, in order to secure the loyalty of the army which he led into Asia, had allowed it a luxury and license foreign to the manners of our forefathers; and in the intervals of leisure those charming and voluptuous lands had easily demoralized the warlike spirit of his soldiers. There it was that an army of the Roman people first learned to indulge in women and drink; to admire statues, paintings, and chased vases, to steal them from private houses and public places, to pillage shrines, and to desecrate everything, both sacred and profane. These soldiers, therefore, after they had won the victory, left nothing to the vanquished. In truth, prosperity tries the souls even of the wise; how then should men of depraved character like these make a moderate use of victory?

XII. As soon as riches came to be held in honour, when glory, dominion, and power followed in their train, virtue began to lose its lustre, poverty to be considered a disgrace, blamelessness to be termed malevolence. Therefore as the result of riches, luxury and greed, united with insolence, took possession of our young manhood. They pillaged, squandered; set little value on their own, coveted the goods of others; they disregarded modesty, chastity, everything human and divine; in short, they were utterly thoughtless and reckless.

It is worth your while, when you look upon houses and villas reared to the size of cities, to pay a visit to the temples of the gods built by our forefathers, most reverent of men. But they adorned the shrines of the gods with piety, their own homes with glory, while from the vanquished they took naught save the power of doing harm. The men of to-day, on the contrary, basest of creatures, with supreme wickedness are robbing our allies of all that those heroes in the hour of victory had left them; they act as though the one and only way to rule were to wrong.

XIII. Why, pray, should I speak of things which are incredible except to those who have seen them, that a host of private men have levelled mountains and built upon the seas? To such men their riches seem to me to have been but a plaything; for while they might have enjoyed them honourably, they made haste to squander them shamefully. Nay more, the passion which arose for lewdness, gluttony, and the other attendants of luxury was equally strong; men played the woman, women offered their chastity for sale; to gratify their palates they scoured land and sea; they slept before they needed sleep; they did not await the coming of hunger or thirst, of cold or of weariness, but all these things their self-indulgence anticipated. Such were the vices that incited the young men to crime, as soon as they had run through their property. Their minds, habituated to evil practices, could not easily refrain from self-indulgence, and so they abandoned themselves the more recklessly to every means of gain as well as of extravagance.

XIV. In a city so great and so corrupt Catiline found it a very easy matter to surround himself, as by a bodyguard, with troops of criminals and reprobates of every kind. For whatever wanton, glutton, or gamester had wasted his patrimony in play, feasting, or debauchery; anyone who had contracted an immense debt that he might buy immunity from disgrace or crime; all, furthermore, from every side who had been convicted of murder or sacrilege, or feared prosecution for their crimes; those, too, whom hand and tongue supported by perjury or the blood of their fellow citizens; finally, all who were hounded by disgrace, poverty, or an evil conscience—all these were nearest and dearest to Catiline. And if any guiltless man did chance to become his friend, daily intercourse and the allurements of vice soon made him as bad or almost as bad as the rest. But most of all Catiline sought the intimacy of the young; their minds, still pliable as they were and easily moulded, were without difficulty ensnared by his wiles. For carefully noting the passion which burned in each, according to his time of life, he found harlots for some or bought dogs and horses for others; in fine, he spared neither expense nor his own decency, provided he could make them submissive and loyal to himself. I am aware that some have believed that the young men who frequented Catiline's house set but little store by their chastity; but that report became current rather for other reasons than because anyone had evidence of its truth.

*   *   *

At no other time has the condition of imperial Rome, as it seems to me, been more pitiable. The whole world, from the rising of the sun to its setting, subdued by her arms, rendered obedience to her; at home there was peace and an abundance of wealth, which mortal men deem the chiefest of blessings. Yet there were citizens who from sheer perversity were bent upon their own ruin and that of their country. For in spite of the two decrees of the senate not one man of all that great number was led by the promised reward to betray the conspiracy, and not a single one deserted Catiline's camp; such was the potency of the malady which like a plague had infected the minds of many of our countrymen.

XXXVII. This insanity was not confined to those who were implicated in the plot, but the whole body of the commons through desire for change favoured the designs of Catiline. In this very particular they seemed to act as the populace usually does; for in every community those who have no means envy the good, exalt the base, hate what is old and established, long for something new, and from disgust with their own lot desire a general upheaval. Amid turmoil and rebellion they maintain themselves without difficulty, since poverty is easily provided for and can suffer no loss. But the city populace in particular acted with desperation for many reasons. To begin with, all who were especially conspicuous for their shamelessness and impudence, those too who had squandered their patrimony in riotous living, finally all whom disgrace or crime had forced to leave home, had all flowed into Rome as into a cesspool. Many, too, who recalled Sulla's victory, when they saw common soldiers risen to the rank of senator, and others become so rich that they feasted and lived like kings, hoped each for himself for like fruits of victory, if he took the field. Besides this, the young men who had maintained a wretched existence by manual labour in the country, tempted by public and private doles had come to prefer idleness in the city to their hateful toil; these, like all the others, battened on the public ills. Therefore it is not surprising that men who were beggars and without character, with illimitable hopes, should respect their country as little as they did themselves. Moreover, those to whom Sulla's victory had meant the proscription of their parents, loss of property, and curtailment of their rights, looked forward in a similar spirit to the issue of a war. Finally, all who belonged to another party than that of the senate preferred to see the government overthrown rather than be out of power themselves. Such, then, was the evil which after many years had returned upon the state.

XXXVIII. For after the tribunician power had been restored in the consulship of Gnaeus Pompeius and Marcus Crassus, various young men, whose age and disposition made them aggressive, attained that high authority; they thereupon began to excite the commons by attacks upon the senate and then to inflame their passions still more by doles and promises, thus making themselves conspicuous and influential. Against these men the greater part of the nobles strove with might and main, ostensibly in behalf of the senate but really for their own aggrandizement. For, to tell the truth in a few words, all who after that time assailed the government used specious pretexts, some maintaining that they were defending the rights of the commons, others that they were upholding the prestige of the senate; but under pretence of the public welfare each in reality was working for his own advancement. Such men showed neither self-restraint nor moderation in their strife, and both parties used their victory ruthlessly.

XXXIX. When, however, Gnaeus Pompeius had been dispatched to wage war against the pirates and against Mithridates, the power of the commons was lessened, while that of the few increased. These possessed the magistracies, the provinces and everything else; being themselves rich and secure against attack, they lived without fear and by resort to the courts terrified the others, in order that while they themselves were in office they might manage the people with less friction. But as soon as the political situation became doubtful, and offered hope of a revolution, then the old controversy aroused their passions anew. If Catiline had been victor in the first battle, or had merely held his own, beyond a doubt great bloodshed and disaster would have fallen upon the state; nor would the victors have been allowed for long to enjoy their success, but when they had been worn out and exhausted, a more powerful adversary would have wrested from them the supreme power and with it their freedom.

Part Three

 THE NEW ERA

The Roman Republic collapsed in two decades of civil war. Caesar's dictatorship had brought a brief glimpse of stability, but his assassination ushered in renewed strife and warfare. A tired and decimated populace had had enough of its own bloodletting. Traditional leadership was discredited and the institutions which had carried the Republic for so long did not survive the crisis. Rome was prepared for a new order, and the civil war produced the man who was prepared to give it to her. When Augustus vanquished Mark Antony in 31 B.C. he eliminated the last rival capable of offering a challenge to his supremacy. He could now undertake the task of reuniting a divided populace and instituting a system which would solidify that unity.

Augustus fitted out his rule with numerous Republican trappings. The system of magistrates and public officials remained intact, as did the senate and the assemblies. Aristocrats continued to hold office and the people continued to cast their ballots. But one-man rule was a fact. Augustus created a new set of appointed officials, planted the seeds of an incipient imperial bureaucracy, and made his wishes known to the senate and the electorate, which duly followed his lead. There were few who would choose to complain. The alternative was chaos and anarchy, which Rome had just experienced and feared to repeat.

Augustus brought along his own panegyrists. Some of the best intellects and literary figures of the period were drawn to the imperial court and exercised their talents on behalf of the regime.

Vergil sang of the coming of a golden age and produced a new epic on Rome's origins: the state was reborn now in a more glorious form under the aegis of Augustus. The more detached poet Horace nonetheless accepted imperial patronage and lauded the new monarch as Jove's own representative on earth. Nor did subsidization of art entail its prostitution. There was genuine feeling of relief and an optimistic outlook for the future. The coming of peace and stability was welcome to common citizen and literary artist alike. Augustus himself left a record of his accomplishments on stone, inscribed and installed by a grateful populace even in far corners of the empire.

The system of Augustus was expanded and solidified by his successors. Tiberius, Caligula, Claudius, and Nero comprised the Julio-Claudian dynasty which endured for more than half a century after Augustus' death. None had the personal popularity of Augustus, but their lengthy combined reigns perpetuated the monarchy and the imperial system. As Tacitus perceptively noted, however, by the time of Augustus' funeral in 14 A.D. there were few Romans left who remembered the dismal days of civil war and anarchy. As the Julio-Claudian dynasty progressed, men took stability for granted and began to concentrate on the disadvantages wrought by monarchy. An unpopular ruler made those disadvantages more conspicuous and called forth criticism and satire. Much of the critical literature was suppressed or circulated only in private; but some has survived. A vicious lampoon on the Emperor Claudius, usually attributed to Seneca, made the rounds after Claudius' death. It called attention to the emperor's follies, his vices, and his cruelties. And in the reign of Nero, the fiery young poet Lucan wrote of the fall of the Republic, reserved praise for shades of Republican heroes, and openly contrasted the freedom of the past with the oppression of his own day. Stability and order were the hallmarks of monarchy; but the system could also produce tyrants, and to some intellectuals the remedy of past disorders had proved worse than the disease which it had cured. This dialogue of the admirers and critics of the early empire forms the substance of the following selections.

Augustus: *Achievements of the Divine Augustus*

Advertisement is always a useful device to promote the acceptance of a new regime. Augustus had his panegyrists in prose and verse. But he also sought more tangible reminders of his benefits and achievements to be observed by the provincial populations. Hence the emperor compiled a record of his deeds which he ordered to be set up in Rome and inscribed on temples in the empire. This is the *Res Gestae Divi Augusti* (*Achievements of the Divine Augustus*), three copies of which, or parts of copies, have been recovered in Galatia in modern Turkey. The document is a unique example of its kind and revealing evidence for the aspects of his rule which Augustus desired to emphasize. The honors voted to the emperor by senate and people receive extensive treatment. Although Augustus insists that he obtained no office or power which did not have Republican precedents, the accumulation of duties and honors obviously signifies that his position was unparalleled in Roman history. As might be expected, he also calls attention to himself as the bringer of peace, the man who finally allowed Rome to close the doors of the temple of Janus. Even more interesting, however, is the fact that Augustus echoes the pride in conquest and expansion so familiar from the Republic. He had healed civil strife, but had also demonstrated Roman might to the barbarian and extended the imperial boundaries to the Danube and elsewhere. The autobiographical portrait he presents is consciously contrived to appeal to traditional sentiments: Augustus not only restored institutions and order; he was the heir of Republican conquerors of the past.

The following selection is from *Res Gestae Divi Augusti,* Secs. 9–13, 25–35; eds. P. A. Brunt and J. M. Moore (London: Oxford University Press, 1967), 23, 25, 31, 33, 35, 37. Reprinted by permission of the publisher.

9 The senate decreed that vows should be undertaken every fifth year by the consuls and priests for my health. In fulfillment of these vows games have frequently been celebrated in my lifetime, sometimes by the four most distinguished colleges of priests, sometimes by the consuls. Moreover, all the citizens, individually and on behalf of their towns, have unanimously and continuously offered prayers at all the *pulvinaria* for my health.

10 My name was inserted in the hymn of the Salii by a decree of the senate, and it was enacted by law that my person should be inviolable for ever and that I should hold the tribunician power for the duration of my life. I declined to be made *pontifex maximus* in the place of my colleague who was still alive, when the people offered me this priesthood which my father had held. Some years later, after the death of the man who had taken the opportunity of civil disturbance to seize it for himself, I received this priesthood, in the consulship of Publius Sulpicius and Gaius Valgius, and such a concourse poured in from the whole of Italy to my election as has never been recorded at Rome before that time.

11 The senate consecrated the altar of Fortuna Redux before the temples of Honour and Virtue at the Porta Capena in honour of my return, and it ordered that the *pontifices* and Vestal virgins should make an annual sacrifice there on the anniversary of my return to the city from Syria in the consulship of Quintus Lucretius and Marcus Vinicius, and it named the day the Augustalia from my *cognomen*.

12 In accordance with the will of the senate some of the praetors and tribunes of the plebs with the consul Quintus Lucretius and the leading men were sent to Campania to meet me, an honour that up to the present day has been decreed to no one besides myself. On my return from Spain and Gaul in the consulship of Tiberius Nero and Publius Quintilius after successfully arranging affairs in those provinces, the senate resolved that an altar of the Augustan Peace should be consecrated next to the Campus Martius in honour of my return, and ordered that the magistrates and priests and Vestal virgins should perform an annual sacrifice there.

13 It was the will of our ancestors that the gateway of Janus Quirinus should be shut when victories had secured peace by

land and sea throughout the whole empire of the Roman people; from the foundation of the city down to my birth, tradition records that it was shut only twice, but while I was the leading citizen the senate resolved that it should be shut on three occasions.

*   *   *

25 I made the sea peaceful and freed it of pirates. In that war I captured about 30,000 slaves who had escaped from their masters and taken up arms against the republic, and I handed them over to their masters for punishment. The whole of Italy of its own free will swore allegiance to me and demanded me as the leader in the war in which I was victorious at Actium. The Gallic and Spanish provinces, Africa, Sicily and Sardinia swore the same oath of allegiance. More than seven hundred senators served under my standards at that time, including eighty-three who previously or subsequently (down to the time of writing) were appointed consuls, and about one hundred and seventy who were appointed priests.

26 I extended the territory of all those provinces of the Roman people on whose borders lay peoples not subject to our government. I brought peace to the Gallic and Spanish provinces as well as to Germany, throughout the area bordering on the Ocean from Cadiz to the mouth of the Elbe. I secured the pacification of the Alps from the district nearest the Adriatic to the Tuscan sea, yet without waging an unjust war on any people. My fleet sailed through the Ocean eastwards from the mouth of the Rhine to the territory of the Cimbri, a country which no Roman had visited before either by land or sea, and the Cimbri, Charydes, Semnones and other German peoples of that region sent ambassadors and sought my friendship and that of the Roman people. At my command and under my auspices two armies were led almost at the same time into Ethiopia and Arabia Felix; vast enemy forces of both peoples were cut down in battle and many towns captured. Ethiopia was penetrated as far as the town of Nabata, which adjoins Meroë; in Arabia the army advanced into the territory of the Sabaeans to the town of Mariba.

27 I added Egypt to the empire of the Roman people. Greater Armenia I might have made a province after its king, Artaxes had been killed, but I preferred, following the model set by our ancestors, to hand over that kingdom to Tigranes, son of King Ar-

tavasdes and grandson of King Tigrancs; Tiberius Nero, who was then my stcpson, carried this out. When the same people later rebelled and went to war, I subdued them through the agency of my son Gaius and handed them over to be ruled by King Ario- barzanes, son of Artabazus King of the Medes, and after his death to his son Artavasdes. When he was killed I sent Tigranes, a scion of the royal Armenian house, to that kingdom. I recovered all the provinces beyond the Adriatic sea towards the east, together with Cyrene, the greater part of them being then occupied by kings. I had previously recovered Sicily and Sardinia which had been seized in the slave war.

28 I founded colonies of soldiers in Africa, Sicily, Macedonia, both Spanish provinces, Achaea, Asia, Syria, Gallia Narbonensis and Pisidia. Italy too has twenty-eight colonies founded by my authority, which were densely populated in my lifetime.

29 By victories over enemies I recovered in Spain and in Gaul, and from the Dalmatians several standards lost by other com- manders. I compelled the Parthians to restore to me the spoils and standards of three Roman armies and to ask as suppliants for the friendship of the Roman people. Those standards I de- posited in the innermost shrine of the temple of Mars the Avenger.

30 The Pannonian peoples, whom the army of the Roman peo- ple never approached before I was the leading citizen, were con- quered through the agency of Tiberius Nero, who was then my stepson and legate; I brought them into the empire of the Roman people, and extended the frontier of Illyricum to the banks of the Danube. When an army of Dacians crossed the Danube, it was defeated and routed under my auspices, and later my army crossed the Danube and compelled the Dacian peoples to submit to the commands of the Roman people.

31 Embassies from kings in India were frequently sent to me; never before had they been seen with any Roman commander. The Bastarnae, Scythians and the kings of the Sarmatians on either side of the river Don, and the kings of the Albanians and the Iberians and the Medes sent embassies to seek our friendship.

32 The following kings sought refuge with me as suppliants: Tiridates, King of Parthia, and later Phraates son of King Phra- atcs; Artavades, King of the Medes; Artaxares, King of the Adia- beni; Dumnobellaunus and Tincommius, Kings of the Britons; Maelo, King of the Sugambri; . . . rus, King of the Marcomanni and Suebi. Phraates, Son of Orodes, King of Parthia, sent all his

sons and grandsons to me in Italy, not that he had been overcome in war, but because he sought our friendship by pledging his children. While I was the leading citizen very many other peoples have experienced the good faith of the Roman people which had never previously exchanged embassies or had friendly relations with the Roman people.

33 The Parthian and Median peoples sent to me ambassadors of their nobility who sought and received kings from me, for the Parthians Vonones, son of King Phraates, grandson of King Orodes, and for the Medes, Ariobarzanes, son of King Artavasdes, grandson of King Ariobarzanes.

34 In my sixth and seventh consulships, after I had extinguished civil wars, and at a time when with universal consent I was in complete control of affairs, I transferred the republic from my power to the dominion of the senate and people of Rome. For this service of mine I was named Augustus by decree of the senate, and the door-posts of my house were publicly wreathed with bay leaves and a civic crown was fixed over my door and a golden shield was set in the Curia Julia, which, as attested by the inscription thereon, was given me by the senate and people of Rome on account of my courage, clemency, justice and piety. After this time I excelled all in influence, although I possessed no more official power than others who were my colleagues in the several magistracies.

35 In my thirteenth consulship the senate, the equestrian order and the whole people of Rome gave me the title of Father of my Country, and resolved that this should be inscribed in the porch of my house and in the Curia Julia and in the Forum Augustum below the chariot which had been set there in my honour by decree of the senate. At the time of writing I am in my seventy-sixth year.

Vergil: The *Fourth Eclogue* and the *Aeneid*

Publius Vergilius Maro (70–19 B.C.) lived through those decades of civil war which saw Italian fields ravaged, property confiscated, and men thrust from their homes. The experience haunted his poetry. A deep humanitarianism, a closeness to the land and to nature infused Vergil's celebration of pastoral scenes and Italian agriculture. His own land was at the mercy of conquering warriors and legions. He could sympathize directly with the pain and burden of the innocent, the neutral, the men who had not taken sides in civil conflict but who had suffered the most: the peace-loving cultivators of the land and property owners who were turned into homeless wanderers and exiles. For such a poet, the coming of peace and the installation of a new order brought genuine rejoicing. Vergil had made his reputation already with the *Eclogues*. The most famous and striking of them, the *Fourth Eclogue*, was written in 40 B.C., shortly after a reconciliation between Augustus and Antony. For the poet that signaled peace and renewed joy. Vergil could envision the inception of a golden age, symbolized by a child soon to be born. Medieval Christians saw the poem as anticipating the birth of Christ. Vergil himself, no doubt, looked forward to an offspring of the union between Antony and the sister of Augustus. But civil war came again and ended with the crushing of Antony and the triumph of Augustus. Vergil was soon brought into Augustus' literary circle by Maecenas, who served as something of a cultural minister for the emperor. Vergil's poetic masterpiece, the *Aeneid*, was an epic poem on Rome's origins and her destiny. It would be foolish to regard it simply as a piece commissioned by Augustus and designed as propaganda for the regime. But the theme harmonized perfectly with the aims of the new order. The greatness of Rome, for Vergil, is part of a divine plan, destined from the beginning. It was to culminate, so Jupiter predicted, in an emperor whose kingdom would be bounded only by the boundaries of the world itself and whose fame would re-echo in the heavens. Rome can leave to others art, science, and philosophy; it is the destiny of Rome to govern, to humble the haughty, protect the weak, and to bring peace to the universe.

The Fourth Eclogue

Sicilian Muse, I would try now a somewhat grander theme.
Shrubberies or meek tamarisks are not for all: but if it's
Forests I sing, may the forests be worthy of a consul.
    Ours is the crowning era foretold in prophecy:
Born of Time, a great new cycle of centuries
Begins. Justice returns to earth, the Golden Age
Returns, and its first-born comes down from heaven above.
Look kindly, chaste Lucina, upon this infant's birth,
For with him shall hearts of iron cease, and hearts of gold
Inherit the whole earth—yes, Apollo reigns now.
And it's while you are consul—you, Pollio—that this glorious
Age shall dawn, the march of its great months begin.
You at our head, mankind shall be freed from its age-long fear,
All stains of our past wickedness being cleansed away.
This child shall enter into the life of the gods, behold them
Walking with antique heroes, and himself be seen of them,
And rule a world made peaceful by his father's virtuous acts.
    Child, your first birthday presents will come from nature's wild—
Small presents: earth will shower you with romping ivy, foxgloves,
Bouquets of gipsy lilies and sweetly-smiling acanthus.
Goats shall walk home, their udders taut with milk, and nobody
Herding them: the ox will have no fear of the lion:
Silk-soft blossom will grow from your very cradle to lap you.
But snakes will die, and so will fair-seeming, poisonous plants.
Everywhere the commons will breathe of spice and incense.
    But when you are old enough to read about famous men
And your father's deeds, to comprehend what manhood means,
Then a slow flush of tender gold shall mantle the great plains,
Then shall grapes hang wild and reddening on thorn-trees,
And honey sweat like dew from the hard bark of oaks.
Yet there'll be lingering traces still of our primal error,
Prompting us to dare the seas in ships, to girdle
Our cities round with walls and break the soil with plough-shares.
A second Argo will carry her crew of chosen heroes,
A second Tiphys steer her. And wars—yes, even wars
There'll be; and great Achilles must sail for Troy again.

Later, when the years have confirmed you in full manhood,
Traders will retire from the sea, from the pine-built vessels
They used for commerce: every land will be self-supporting.
The soil will need no harrowing, the vine no pruning-knife;
And the tough ploughman may at last unyoke his oxen.
We shall stop treating wool with artificial dyes,
For the ram himself in his pasture will change his fleece's colour,
Now to a charming purple, now to a saffron hue,
And grazing lambs will dress themselves in coats of scarlet.
    "Run, looms, and weaves this future!"—thus have the Fates spoken,
In unison with the unshakeable intent of Destiny.
    Come soon, dear child of the gods, Jupiter's great viceroy!
Come soon—the time is near—to begin your life illustrious!
Look how the round and ponderous globe bows to salute you,
The lands, the stretching leagues of sea, the unplumbed sky!
Look how the whole creation exults in the age to come!
    If but the closing days of a long life were prolonged
For me, and I with breath enough to tell your story,
Oh then I should not be worsted at singing by Thracian Orpheus
Or Linus—even though Linus were backed by Calliope
His mother, and Orpheus by his father, beauteous Apollo.
Should Pan compete with me, and Arcady judge us, even
Pan, great Pan, with Arcadian judges, would lose the contest.
    Begin, dear babe, and smile at your mother to show you know her—
This is the tenth month now, and she is sick of waiting.
Begin, dear babe. The boy who does not smile at his mother
Will never deserve to sup with a god or sleep with a goddess.

                    *   *   *

The Aeneid

Fear no more, Cytherea. Take comfort, for your people's
Destiny is unaltered; you shall behold the promised
City walls of Lavinium, and exalt great-hearted Aeneas
Even to the starry skies. I have not changed my mind.
I say it now—for I know these cares constantly gnaw you—
And show you further into the secret book of fate:
Aeneas, mightily warring in Italy, shall crush
Proud tribes, to establish city walls and a way of life,
Till a third summer has seen him reigning in Latium

And winter thrice passed over his camp in the conquered land.
His son Ascanius, whose surname is now Iulus—
Ilus it was, before the realm of Ilium fell—
Ascanius for his reign shall have full thirty years
With all their wheeling months; shall move the kingdom from
Lavinium and make Long Alba his sure stronghold.
Here for three hundred years shall rule the dynasty
Of Hector, until a priestess and queen of Trojan blood,
With child by Mars, shall presently give birth to twin sons.
Romulus, then, gay in the coat of the tawny she-wolf
Which suckled him, shall succeed to power and found the city
Of Mars and with his own name endow the Roman nation.
To these I set no bounds, either in space or time;
Unlimited power I give them. Even the spiteful Juno,
Who in her fear now troubles the earth, the sea and the sky,
Shall think better of this and join me in fostering
The cause of the Romans, the lords of creation, the togaed people.
Thus it is written. An age shall come, as the years glide by,
When the children of Troy shall enslave the children of Agamemnon,
Of Diomed and Achilles, and rule in conquered Argos.
From the fair seed of Troy there shall be born a Caesar—
Julius, his name derived from great Iulus—whose empire
Shall reach to the ocean's limits, whose fame shall end in the stars.
He shall hold the East in fee; one day, cares ended, you shall
Receive him into heaven; him also will mortals pray to.
Then shall the age of violence be mellowing into peace:
Venerable Faith, and the Home, with Romulus and Remus,
Shall make the laws; the grim, steel-welded gates of War
Be locked; and within, on a heap of armaments, a hundred
Bronzen knots tying his hands behind him, shall sit
Growling and bloody-mouthed the godless spirit of Discord.
   So Jupiter spoke, and sent Mercury down from on high

*   *   *

   Listen, for I will show you your destiny, setting forth
The fame that from now shall attend the seed of Dardanus,
The posterity that awaits you from an Italian marriage—
Illustrious souls, one day to come in for our Trojan name.
That young man there—do you see him? who leans on an untipped spear,
Has been allotted the next passage to life, and first of
All these will ascend to earth, with Italian blood in his veins;
He is Silvius, an Alban name, and destined to be your last child,
The child of your late old age by a wife, Lavinia, who shall
Bear him in sylvan surroundings, a king and the father of kings

Through whom our lineage shall rule in Alba Longa.
Next to him stands Procas, a glory to the Trojan line;
Then Capys and Numitor, and one who'll revive your own name—
Silvius Aeneas, outstanding alike for moral rectitude
And prowess in warfare, if ever he comes to the Alban throne.
What fine young men they are! Look at their stalwart bearing,
The oak leaves that shade their brows—decorations for saving life!
These shall found your Nomentum, Gabii and Fidenae,
These shall rear on the hills Collatia's citadel,
Pometii, and the Fort of Inuus, Bola and Cora—
All nameless sites at present, but then they shall have these names.
Further, a child of Mars shall go to join his grandsire—
Romulus, born of the stock of Assaracus by his mother,
Ilia. Look at the twin plumes upon his helmet's crest,
Mars' cognisance, which marks him out for the world of earth!
His are the auguries, my son, whereby great Rome
Shall rule to the ends of the earth, shall aspire to the highest achievement,
Shall ring the seven hills with a wall to make one city,
Blessed in her breed of men: as Cybele, wearing her turreted
Crown, is charioted round the Phrygian cities, proud of
Her brood of gods, embracing a hundred of her children's children—
Heaven-dwellers all, all tenants of the realm above.
Now bend your gaze this way, look at that people there!
They are *your* Romans. Caesar is there and all Ascanius'
Posterity, who shall pass beneath the arch of day.
And here, here is the man, the promised one you know of—
Caesar Augustus, son of a god, destined to rule
Where Saturn ruled of old in Latium, and there
Bring back the age of gold: his empire shall expand
Past Garamants and Indians to a land beyond the zodiac
And the sun's yearly path, where Atlas the sky-bearer pivots
The wheeling heavens, embossed with fiery stars, on his shoulder.
Even now the Caspian realm, the Crimean country
Tremble at oracles of the gods predicting his advent,
And the seven mouths of the Nile are in a lather of fright.
Not even Hercules roved so far and wide over earth,
Although he shot the bronze-footed deer, brought peace to the woods of
Erymanthus, subdued Lerna with the terror of his bow;
Nor Bacchus, triumphantly driving his team with vines for reins,
His team of tigers down from Mount Nysa, travelled so far.
Do we still hesitate, then, to enlarge our courage by action?
Shrink from occupying the territory of Ausonia?
Who is that in the distance, bearing the hallows, crowned with
A wreath of olive? I recognise—grey hair and hoary chin—

That Roman king who, called to high power from humble Cures,
A town in a poor area, shall found our system of law
And thus refound our city. The successor of Numa, destined
To shake our land out of its indolence, stirring men up to fight
Who have grown unadventurous and lost the habit of victory,
Is Tullus. After him shall reign the too boastful Ancus,
Already over-fond of the breath of popular favour.
Would you see the Tarquin kings, and arrogant as they, Brutus
The avenger, with the symbols of civic freedom he won back?
He shall be first to receive consular rank and its power of
Life and death: when his sons awake the dormant conflict,
Their father, a tragic figure, shall call them to pay the extreme
Penalty, for fair freedom's sake. However posterity
Look on that deed, patriotism shall prevail and love of
Honour. See over there the Decii, the Drusi, Torquatus
With merciless axe, Camillus with the standards he recovered.
See those twin souls, resplendent in duplicate armour: now
They're of one mind, and shall be as long as the Underworld holds them;
But oh, if ever they reach the world above, what warfare,
What battles and what carnage will they create between them—
Caesar descending from Alpine strongholds, the fort of Monoecus,
His son-in-law Pompey lined up with an Eastern army against him.
Lads, do not harden yourselves to face such terrible wars!
Turn not your country's hand against your country's heart!
You, be the first to renounce it, my son of heavenly lineage,
You be the first to bury the hatchet! . . .
That one shall ride in triumph to the lofty Capitol,
The conqueror of Corinth, renowned for the Greeks he has slain.
That one shall wipe out Argos and Agamemnon's Mycenae,
Destroying an heir of Aeacus, the seed of warrior Achilles,
Avenging his Trojan sires and the sacrilege done to Minerva.
Who could leave unnoticed the glorious Cato, Cossus,
The family of the Gracchi, the two Scipios—thunderbolts
In war and death to Libya; Fabricius, who had plenty
In poverty; Serranus, sowing his furrowed fields?
Fabii, where do you lead my lagging steps? O Fabius,
The greatest, you the preserver of Rome by delaying tactics!
Let others fashion from bronze more lifelike, breathing images—
For so they shall—and evoke living faces from marble;
Others excel as orators, others track with their instruments
The planets circling in heaven and predict when stars will appear.
But, Romans, never forget that government is your medium!
Be this your art:—to practise men in the habit of peace,
Generosity to the conquered, and firmness against aggressors.

Horace: Odes

Like Vergil, Quintus Horatius Flaccus (65–8 B.C.) witnessed the grim years of anarchy and civil war which preceded the Augustan restoration. Horace indeed experienced directly the battlefield and the confiscation of property. He had served in the ranks of Augustus' enemies in the 40's B.C., but fled the fighting and pursued a wiser course after the victory of Augustus. Vergil himself introduced Horace to Maecenas and into the emperor's literary entourage. Again, however, the poet is not to be seen as a salaried tool mouthing the propaganda of the court. Horace was proud of his independence; he bristled at suggestions that he was merely a spokesman for official policy. He declined official posts offered by Augustus and preferred idleness, independence, the carefree existence of the gay bachelor, characteristics that emerge very clearly in his poetry. Horace had praise for the emperor, but for reasons that one need not doubt were genuine. Augustus is portrayed as the conveyer of universal peace, as the vigilant protector and defender of the empire. For a man like Horace who asked only for the simple life and rustic joys, the Augustan revival of antique simplicity was most congenial. At the same time, the Republican themes which boasted of expansion and triumph and which are echoed in Augustus' Res Gestae may be found in Horace as well. He recounts the story of Regulus, the Roman warrior against Carthage who represents the ancient martial virtues. Those virtues too were revived, in Horace's eyes, by Augustus, who once more turned Roman arms against the foreigner. The emperor is praised for humbling the Parthian, subduing the barbarian, and expanding the realm. Even where praise is effusive it is not irrelevant. Augustus is not depicted as a monarch or a god, but the heir of Roman champions, the favorite of Jupiter, and the agent of heaven, destined to rule the world for the benefit of mankind.

The following selections are from Horace, Odes, Book I, Odes 2, 12; Book III, Odes 5, 14; Book IV, Odes 5, 14, 15; trans.

Casper J. Kraemer, Jr. in *The Complete Works of Horace* (New York: The Modern Library, 1936), 129–31, 144–46, 227–29, 245–46, 281–82, 298–301. Reprinted by permission of the publisher.

Enough of snow and hail in tempest dire
Have poured on earth, while heaven's eternal sire
With red right arm at his own temples hurled
His thunders, and alarmed a guilty world,

Lest Pyrrha should again with plaintive cries
Behold the monsters of the deep arise,
When to the mountain summit Proteus drove
His sea-born herd, and where the woodland dove

Late perched his wonted seat, the scaly hood
Entangled hung upon the topmost wood,
And every timorous native of the plain,
High floating, swam amid the boundless main.

We saw, pushed backward to his native source,
The yellow Tiber roll his rapid course;
With impious ruin threatening Vesta's fane,
And the great monuments of Numa's reign;

With grief and rage while Ilia's bosom glows,
Boastful, for her revenge, his waters rose;
But now the uxorious river glides away,
So Jove commands, smooth-winding to the sea.

And yet, less numerous by their parents' crimes,
Our sons shall hear, shall hear to latest times,
Of Roman arms with civil gore imbrued
Which better had the Persian subdued.

Among her guardian gods, what pitying power
To raise her sinking state shall Rome implore,
Shall her own hallowed virgins' earnest prayer
Harmonious charm offended Vesta's ire?

To whom shall Jove assign to purge away
The guilty deed? Come, then, bright god of day,
But gracious veil thy shoulder beaming bright—
Oh! veil in clouds the unsufferable light.

O come, sweet queen of smiles, while round thee rove,
On wanton wing, the powers of mirth and love.
O hither, Mars, thine aspect gracious bend,
And powerful thy neglected race defend.

Parent of Rome, amidst the rage of fight
Sated with scenes of blood, thy fierce delight—
Thou, whom the polished helm, the noise of arms,
And the stern soldiers' frown with transport warms:

Oh thou, fair Maia's winged son appear,
And human shape in prime of manhood wear;
Declared the guardian of the imperial state,
Divine avenger of great Caesar's fate.

Oh! late return to heaven and may thy reign
With lengthened blessings fill thy wide domain!
Nor let thy people's crimes provoke thy flight
On air swift rising to the realms of light.

Great prince and father of the state, receive
The noblest triumphs which thy Rome can give;
Nor let the Parthian, with unpunished pride,
Beyond his bounds, O Caesar, dare to ride.

       *   *   *

Clio, what man, what hero, or what God
   Shall wake thy lyre—thy flute with sweetness thrill;
Whose name shall playful echo send abroad
   In whispers from her hill?

Whether on Helicon's umbrageous side,
   Or Pindus' height, or Haemus' peak of snow,
Whence suddenly, self-wooed, the forests glide
   As Orpheus' numbers flow.

And by the art his goddess mother gave
   He bids the rivers pause, the winds delay;
The oaks, as in gigantic strength they wave,
   Hear and his lute obey.

Father Supreme, of earth and ocean King,
   Ruler of all things human and divine,
Guide of the world, whose praises can I sing
   Before I utter thine?

None greater than thyself has sprung from thee;
   None like, none second to thy power is found;
Yet Pallas next, thy wondrous progeny,
   Is after thee renown'd.

Victorious Bacchus, how can I abstain
   To laud thy name? Or thine, thou virgin foe
Of the fierce forest tribes? Or thine refrain,
   Lord of the fatal bow?

Alcides sing I, and each royal twin,
　The wild-steed tamer and the arm of might;
When on the mariners their stars begin
　To pour their silver light,

Down from the cliffs the showers of spray distil,
　The winds are lulled, the clouds obedient flee;
The mountain waves, subservient to their will,
　Sink down upon the sea.

Shall Romulus, or Numa's tranquil reign,
　Afford the fittest theme to celebrate?
Shall Tarquin's haughty rule awake the strain,
　Or Cato's noble fate?

To Regulus, the Scauri and (of life
　Too prodigal on Cannae's bloody field)
Paulus, and old Fabricius, verses rife
　With grace their fame shall yield.

Stern poverty and the ancestral farm
　Trained these, and Curius rough with tangled hair,
For war; and nerved Camillus' mighty arm
　The battle's toil to dare.

As spreads a tree, so grows Marcellus' fame
　With every year; the Julian orb afar
Gleams bright, as when the moonbeam's lambent flame
　Outshines each minor star.

Father and guardian of the human race,
　Offspring of Saturn, thine by destiny,
Great Caesar's charge. Thou art supreme; his place
　Second to none but thee:

Whether when Parthia threatened with her hosts
　Fair Latium, their repulse his triumph gained;
Or India's tribes, or hordes from China's coasts
　His mighty hand restrained.

On thy behalf still may he rule the world;
　Shake with thy ponderous car the worlds above;
By thee the avenging bolts of heaven be hurled
　On each polluted grove!

＊　　　　　＊　　　　　＊

Jove rules the skies, his thunder wielding:

Augustus Caesar, thou on earth shalt be
  Enthroned a present Deity;
Britons and Parthian hordes to Rome their proud necks yielding.

Woe to the Senate that endures to see
  (O fire extinct of old nobility!)
The soldier dead to honor and to pride
  Ingloriously abide
Grey-headed mate of a Barbarian bride,
Freeman of Rome beneath a Median King!

Woe to the land that fears to fling
Its curse, not ransom, to the slave
Forgetful of the shield of Mars,
Of Vesta's unextinguished flame,
Of Roman garb, of Roman name;
The base unpitied slave who dares
From Rome his forfeit life to crave!
In vain;—Immortal Jove still reigns on high:
Still breathes in Roman hearts the Spirit Liberty.

With warning voice of stern rebuke
Thus Regulus the Senate shook;
He saw, prophetic, in far days to come,
The heart corrupt, and future doom of Rome.
"These eyes," he cried, "these eyes have seen
Unbloodied swords from warriors torn,
And Roman standards nailed in scorn
  On Punic shrines obscene;
Have seen the hands of free-born men
Wrenched back and bound; th' unguarded gate;
And fields our war laid desolate
By Romans tilled again.
What! will the gold-enfranchised slave
Return more loyal and more brave?
  Ye heap but loss on crime!
The wool that Cretan dyes distain
Can ne'er its virgin hue regain;
And valour fallen and disgraced
Revives not in a coward breast
  Its energy sublime.
The stag released from hunter's toils
From the dread sight of man recoils.
Is he more brave than when of old
He ranged his forest free? Behold

In him your soldier. He has knelt
To faithless foes; he too has felt
The knotted cord; and crouched beneath
    Fear, not of shame, but Death.
He sued for peace, tho' vowed to war!
Will such men, girt in arms once more,
Dash headlong on the Punic shore?
No! they will buy their craven lives
With Punic scorn and Punic gyves.
O mighty Carthage, rearing high
Thy fame upon our infamy,
A city, aye, an empire built
On Roman ruins, Roman guilt."

From the chaste kiss and wild embrace
Of wife and babes he turned his face,
    A man self-doomed to die;
Then bent his manly brow, in scorn,
Resolved, relentless, sad, but stern,
    To earth, all silently;
Till counsel never heard before
Had nerved each wavering Senator;
Till flushed each cheek with patriot shame,
And surging rose the loud acclaim;—
Then, from his weeping friends, in haste,
To exile and to death he passed.

He knew the tortures that Barbaric hate
Had stored for him. Exulting in his fate
    With kindly hand he waved away
    The crowds that strove his course to stay,

He passed from all, as when in days of yore,
    His judgment given, thro' client throngs he pressed
    In glad Venafrian fields to seek his rest,
Or Greek Tarentum on the Southern shore.

       *   *   *

Of late we spake how Caesar sought,
Like Hercules, the laurels fraught
With death—To-day, ye folk of Rome,
From Spain he comes triumphant home.

Rejoicing in her peerless spouse
His wife shall go and pay her vows,

With her our hero's sister too,
And, decked with votive fillets due,

The dames of Rome their thanks to pour
For sons and daughters safe once more.
O youths and wedded girls, take care
To utter words of omen fair!

This day shall be in truth a day
Of joy to hunt black care away;
No mobs I dread, nor death by sword,
While Caesar o'er the earth is lord.

Bring wreaths and perfumes, and a jar
That can recall the Marsic war,
And pitcher be, that 'scaped the hands
Of Spartacus' marauding bands.

And bid Neaera, sweet-voiced maid,
Her scented tresses quickly braid;
But if her porter makes delay—
That surly menial—come away!

Hairs growing grey compose a mind
To feuds and quarrels once inclined;
When Plancus ruled and I was hot
And young, I would have brooked it not.

*   *   *

God-Given guardian of Quirinus' sons,
    The sacred Senate holds thy promise dear;
Return, return; too long his absence runs
    Who spake of brief delay and is not here.

Restore to Rome the radiance of that face
    Which, smiling on us like the budding year,
Can lend to gracious day a novel grace,
    And gift the sunshine with a warmer cheer:

For as some mother hungering for her son—
    Fast bound beyond the far Carpathian swell
By jealous gales till all the year be done,
    In exile from the home that loves him well,—

Calls him with vows and prayers and augur's art,
    Her eyes still set toward the sinuous sand,
So from a grateful people's faithful heart
    A cry for Caesar echoes through the land.

For safe the cattle range the peaceful mead,—
    Ceres the mead and glad abundance bless;
O'er bloodless seas the flying galleys speed;
    And faith is fearful of unfaithfulness.

Our homes are pure and happy, every one;
    Good laws, good customs cleanse our leprosies;
The father's face is imaged in the son;
    Immediate vengeance follows hard on vice.

Who recks of dwellers in the Scythian snows?
    Who dreads the Mede? Who fears, if Caesar reign,
Yon savage brood the Teuton forest knows,
    Or who is troubled for the war with Spain?

Each sees the sun down in his native glen,
    There wedding widower elm and tender vine;
Then blithely hies him homeward, and again
    Crowns his glad cup and bids thee bless the wine.

Thee with all prayer, with all libation thee,
    Thee in the number of his Lares set
He worships; so Hellenic piety
    To Castor and Alcides paid its debt.

Good chief, with years of joy thy country dower!
    This at the dawn of days not yet begun
Dry-lipped we pray; and thus in wassail hour
    When couched in ocean sleeps the weary sun.

          *   *   *

How shall the senate, how shall Rome
On sculptured bust, or history's page, record
Thy virtues, Caesar, and their just reward
Stamped on the heart of ages yet to come?
Greatest of chiefs where'er the Lord of Day
Levels o'er peopled shores his morning ray!

Strangers to Roman law till now
The rude Vindelici have learned to bow
To Caesar's warlike might. His sword,
Wielded by Drusus, quelled the Breunian horde,
When Alpine citadels in ashes laid
Saw Rome in blood avenged by slaughter thrice repaid.

Claudius by happy auspice led
Through Rhaetian ranks his onset sped;

Conspicuous in the field of blood,
With what fell ruin he pursued,
Unsated still, that giant brood
Who dared a patriot's death to die
   Martyrs to liberty.

Fierce 'mid the living and the dead,
O'er flaming plains he spurred his steed blood-red;
So southern storms the restless billows smite
When the sad Pleiads, rising through the night,
From bursting clouds send forth their baleful light;
   Or so, in Daunia's ancient realm
   Bull-headed Aufidus amain
Rolls down his raging flood to overwhelm
The harvest ripening on the Apulian plain.

Thus through the Rhaetian's steel array
In front, in rear, young Claudius mowed his way.
On the red earth in serried ranks they lie,
And yield to Rome a bloodless victory.
Thine were the hosts, the counsel, and design,
Caesar! The tutelary gods were thine.
Since that proud day when Alexandria's port
Her vacant halls and her deserted court
Lay'd at thy feet—since that auspicious day
Our stubborn foes a master's hand obey.
   For three long lustres, reconciled,
On noble deeds benignant Fortune smiled,
Then gave to Rome the boon long sought in vain,
The grace, the glory of a peaceful reign.

The proud Iberian, slow to yield,
The Scythians flying o'er the field,
The monster-teeming seas that roar
Round distant Britain's rock-bound shore,
The Gaul in peril unalarmed,
Sygambri peaceful and disarmed,
The Nile that hides his mystic source,
Ister, and Tigris' headlong course,
The Median in his mountain home,
Wondering, adore in thee, Caesar, the shield of Rome.

*　　　　*　　　　*

On siege and battlefield I mused,
   Of martial themes I wished to sing,

But Phoebus chid—my lyre refused
  To speak, and mute was every string;
He bade me furl my little sails,
Nor rashly tempt Tyrrhenian gales.

'Tis thine, O Caesar, to restore
  To wasted fields their wealth of corn;
And standards that we lost of yore,—
  From haughty Parthia's columns torn,—
Bring back in triumph to our shrine,
Of Jupiter Capitoline.

Beneath thy sway we live in peace,
  The double gates of Janus close,
Outbursts of vagrant license cease,
  And all is order and repose;
Thy hand that stays the people's crimes
Restores the arts of olden times:

Arts which have spread the Latin name,
  Increased the might of Italy,
Founded the empire's matchless fame
  And all embracing majesty,
Till they have spanned the earth's extent
From sunset to the Orient.

While we have Caesar at our head,
  Serene custodian of the State,
No civil fury shall we dread,
  Nor feuds that cities desolate;
The rage that fires barbarian hordes
Shall never sharpen Roman swords.

Not they who dwell upon its banks
  And the deep Danube's waters drink,
No faithless Parthian's quivered ranks,
  No natives of the Tanais' lake,
The Julian edicts dare to break.

These themes I leave: the lot be mine
  On common and on festal days,
With Bacchus' gifts of flowers and wine,
  To mingle my congenial lays,—
And while our wives and children share
In offerings of peace and prayer,

We'll, like our fathers, celebrate—
In songs that blend with Lydian pipes—
The men in simple virtues great,
Our captains of the ancient types;
Anchises, Troy, our themes shall be,
And genial Venus' progeny.

The Pumpkinification of Claudius

The successors of Augustus did not enjoy his popularity
or his reputation. Tiberius was dour and morose, unable to
get along with the Roman aristocracy. Caligula was unstable and given to megalomania. Claudius was personally
unattractive and carried the image of weakness and foolishness. Nero was more interested in artistry and charioteering
than in the governing of empire. Under these rulers the less
appealing features of monarchy became more evident. It
was not easy or safe to publish open criticism of the emperors, but time has preserved one piece which suggests the
type of clandestine literature that may have circulated. The
Apocolocyntosis Divi Claudii (Pumpkinification of Claudius)
is included among the manuscripts of Seneca, the Stoic philosopher and adviser and tutor to the Emperor Nero.
Whether Seneca actually wrote it cannot be proved and does
not warrant speculation here. It was evidently published after
Claudius' death and in the succeeding reign, perhaps in the
60's A.D. The tract is an amusing but brutal satire on the
funeral and deification of Claudius. The emperor is brought
to heaven to be judged by the gods who must determine
his fate. Among those who judge him is the now deified
Augustus, who recounts his crimes and regards him as the
perverter of all that the Augustan system represented. No
opportunity is missed to lampoon Claudius' physical characteristics and personality, including his shambling gait, his
mumbling speech, his excessive fondness for judicial details,
his gambling habits, his Gallic origins, his weakness for
freedmen, and his reckless cruelties. Naturally Claudius is
cast out of heaven, then condemned to rattle dice in an

inconvenient box, and, with a final touch of irony, becomes
slave to a freedman.

The following selection is from *Apocolocyntosis*, Secs. 5–15,
trans. W. H. D. Rouse in *Petronius, Seneca, Apocolocyntosis*
(Cambridge, Mass.: Harvard University Press, 1956), 379–405.
Reprinted by permission of the publisher and *The Loeb Classical
Library*.

What happened next on earth it is mere waste of time
to tell, for you know it all well enough, and there is no fear of
your ever forgetting the impression which that public rejoicing
made on your memory. No one forgets his own happiness. What
happened in heaven you shall hear: for proof please apply to my
informant. Word comes to Jupiter that a stranger had arrived, a
man well set up, pretty grey; he seemed to be threatening something, for he wagged his head ceaselessly; he dragged the right
foot. They asked him what nation he was of; he answered something in a confused mumbling voice: his language they did not
understand. He was no Greek and no Roman, nor of any known
race. On this Jupiter bids Hercules go and find out what country
he comes from; you see Hercules had travelled over the whole
world, and might be expected to know all the nations in it. But
Hercules, the first glimpse he got, was really much taken aback,
although not all the monsters in the world could frighten him;
when he saw this new kind of object, with its extraordinary gait,
and the voice of no terrestrial beast, but such as you might hear in
the leviathans of the deep, hoarse and inarticulate, he thought his
thirteenth labour had come upon him. When he looked closer, the
thing seemed to be a kind of man. Up he goes, then, and says
what your Greek finds readiest to his tongue:

Who art thou, and what thy people? Who thy parents, where thy home?

Claudius was delighted to find literary men up there, and began to hope there might be some corner for his own historical
works. So he caps him with another Homeric verse, explaining
that he was Caesar:

Breezes wafted me from Ilion unto the Ciconian land.

But the next verse was more true, and no less Homeric:

Thither come, I sacked a city, slew the people every one.

He would have taken in poor simple Hercules, but that Our Lady of Malaria was there, who left her temple and came alone with him: all the other gods he had left at Rome. Quoth she,

> The fellow's tale is nothing but lies. I have lived with him all these years, and I tell you, he was born at Lyons. You behold a fellow-burgess of Marcus. As I say, he was born at the sixteenth milestone from Vienne, a native Gaul. So of course he took Rome, as a good Gaul ought to do. I pledge you my word that in Lyons he was born, where Licinus was king so many years. But you that have trudged over more roads than any muleteer that plies for hire, you must have come across the people of Lyons, and you must know that it is a far cry from Xanthus to the Rhone.

At this point Claudius flared up and expressed his wrath with as big a growl as he could manage. What he said nobody understood; as a matter of fact, he was ordering my lady of Fever to be taken away, and making that sign with his trembling hand (which was always steady enough for that, if for nothing else) by which he used to decapitate men. He had ordered her head to be chopped off. For all the notice the others took of him, they might have been his own freedmen.

Then Hercules said, "You just listen to me, and stop playing the fool. You have come to the place where the mice nibble iron. Out with the truth, and look sharp, or I'll knock your quips and quiddities out of you." Then to make himself all the more awful, he strikes an attitude and proceeds in his most tragic vein:

> Declare with speed what spot you claim by birth,
> Or with this club fall stricken to the earth!
> This club hath ofttimes slaughtered haughty kings!
> Why mumble unintelligible things?
> What land, what tribe produced that shaking head?
> Declare it! On my journey when I sped
> Far to the Kingdom of the triple King,
> And from the Main Hesperian did bring
> The goodly cattle to the Argive town,

There I beheld a mountain looking down
Upon two rivers: this the Sun espies
Right opposite each day he doth arise.
Hence, mighty Rhone, thy rapid torrents flow,
And Arar, much in doubt which way to go,
Ripples along the banks which shallow roll.
Say, is this land, the nurse that bred thy soul?

These lines he delivered with much spirit and a bold front. All the same, he was not quite master of his wits, and had some fear of a blow from the fool. Claudius, seeing a mighty man before him, saw things looked serious and understood that here he had not quite the same pre-eminence as at Rome, where no one was his equal: the Gallic cock was worth most on his own dunghill. So this is what he was thought to say, as far as could be made out:

I did hope, Hercules, bravest of all the gods, that you would take my part with the rest, and if I should need a voucher, I meant to name you who know me so well. Do but call it to mind, how it was I used to sit in judgment before your temple whole days together during July and August. You know what miseries I endured there, in hearing the lawyers plead day and night. If you had fallen amongst these, you may think yourself very strong, but you would have found it worse than the sewers of Augeas: I drained out more filth than you did. But since I want . . .

* * *

No wonder you have forced your way into the Senate House: no bars or bolts can hold against you. Only do say what species of god you want the fellow to be made. An Epicurean god he cannot be: for they have no troubles and cause none. A Stoic, then? How can he be globular, as Varro says, without a head or any other projection? There *is* in him something of the Stoic god, as I can see now: he has neither heart nor head. Upon my word, if he had asked this boon from Saturn, he would not have got it, though he kept up Saturn's feast all the year round, a truly Saturnalian prince. A likely thing he will get it from Jove, whom he condemned for incest as far as in him lay: for he killed his son-in-law Silanus, because Silanus had a sister, a most charming girl, called Venus by all the world, and he preferred to call her Juno. Why, you say, I want to know why, his own sister? Read your books, stupid: you may go half-way at Athens, the whole way at Alexandria. Because the mice lick meal at Rome, you say. Is this creature to mend our crooked ways? What goes on in his own closet he knows not; and now he searches the regions of the sky, wants to be a god. Is it not enough that he has a temple in Britain, that savages worship him and pray to him as a god, so that they may find a fool to have mercy upon them?

At last it came into Jove's head, that while strangers were in the House it was not lawful to speak or debate. "My lords and gentlemen," said he, "I gave you leave to ask questions, and you have made a regular farmyard of the place. Be so good as to keep the rules of the House. What will this person think of us, whoever he is?" So Claudius was led out, and the first to be asked his opinion was Father Janus: he had been made consul elect for the afternoon of the next first of July, being as shrewd a man as you could find on a summer's day: for he could see, as they say, before and behind. He made an eloquent harangue, because his life was passed in the forum, but too fast for the notary to take down. That is why I give no full report of it, for I don't want to change the words he used. He said a great deal of the majesty of the gods, and how the honour ought not to be given away to every Tom, Dick, or Harry. "Once," said he,

it was a great thing to become a god; now you have made it a farce. Therefore, that you may not think I am speaking against one person instead of the general custom, I propose that from this day forward the godhead be given to none of those who eat the fruits of the earth, or whom mother earth doth nourish. After this bill has been read a third time, whosoever is made, said, or portrayed to be god, I vote he be delivered over to the bogies, and at the next public show be flogged with a birch amongst the new gladiators.

The next to be asked was Diespiter, son of Vica Pota, he also being consul elect, and a moneylender; by this trade he made a living, used to sell rights of citizenship in a small way. Hercules trips me up to him daintily, and tweaks him by the ear. So he uttered his opinion in these words:

Inasmuch as the blessed Claudius is akin to the blessed Augustus, and also to the blessed Augusta, his grandmother, whom he ordered to be made a goddess, and whereas he far surpasses all mortal men in wisdom, and seeing that it is for the public good that there be some one able to join Romulus in devouring boiled turnips, I propose that from this day forth blessed Claudius be a god, to enjoy that honour with all its appurtenances in as full a degree as any other before him, and that a note to that effect be added to Ovid's Metamorphoses.

The meeting was divided, and it looked as though Claudius was to win the day. For Hercules saw his iron was in the fire, trotted here and trotted there, saying, "Don't deny me; I make a point of the matter. I'll do as much for you again, when you like; you roll my log, and I'll roll yours: one hand washes another."

Then arose the blessed Augustus when his turn came, and spoke with much eloquence. "I call you to witness, my lords and gentlemen," said he,

that since the day I was made a god I have never uttered one word. I always mind my own business. But now I can keep on the mask no longer, nor conceal the sorrow which shame makes all the greater. Is it for this I have made peace by land and sea? For this have I calmed intestine wars? For this, laid a firm foundation of law for Rome, adorned it with buildings, and all that—my lords, words fail me; there are none can rise to the height of my indignation. I must borrow that saying of the eloquent Messala Corvinus, I am ashamed of my authority. This man, my lords, who looks as though he could not hurt a fly, used to chop off heads as easily as a dog sits down. But why should I speak of all those men, and such men? There is no time to lament for public disasters, when one has so many private sorrows to think of. I leave that, therefore, and say only this; for even if my sister knows no Greek, I do: The knee is nearer than the shin. This man you see, who for so many years has been masquerading under my name, has done me the favour of murdering two Julias, great-granddaughters of mine, one by cold steel and one by starvation; and one great-grandson, L. Silanus—see, Jupiter, whether he had a case against him (at least it is your own if you will be fair). Come tell me, blessed Claudius, why of all those you killed, both men and women, without a hearing, why you did not hear their side of the case first, before putting them to death? Where do we find that custom? It is not done in heaven. Look at Jupiter: all these years he has been king, and never did more than once to break Vulcan's leg,

Whom seizing by the foot he cast from the threshold of the sky,

and once he fell in a rage with his wife and strung her up: did he do any killing? You killed Messalina, whose great-uncle I was no less than yours. "I don't know," did you say? Curse you! that is just it: not to know was worse than to kill. Caligula he went on persecuting even when he was dead. Caligula murdered his father-in-law, Claudius his son-in-law to boot. Caligula would not have Crassus' son called Great; Claudius gave him his name back, and took away his head. In one family he destroyed Crassus Magnus, Scribonia, the Tristionias, Assario, noble though they were; Crassus indeed such a fool that he might have been emperor. Is this he you want now to make a god? Look at his body, born under the wrath of heaven! In fine, let him say the three words quickly, and he may have me for a slave. God! who will worship this god, who will believe in him? While you make gods of such as he, no one will believe you to be gods. To be brief, my lords: if I have lived honourably among you, if I have never given plain speech to any, avenge my wrongs. This is my motion:

then he read out his amendment, which he had committed to writing:

Inasmuch as the blessed Claudius murdered his father-in-law Appius Silanus, his two sons-in-law, Pompeius Magnus and L. Silanus, Crassus Frugi his daughter's father-in-law, as like him as two eggs in a basket, Scribonia his daughter's mother-in-law, his wife Messalina, and others too numerous to mention; I propose that strong measures be taken against him, that he be allowed no delay of process, that immediate sentence of banishment be passed on him, that he be deported from heaven within thirty days, and from Olympus within thirty hours.

This motion was passed without further debate. Not a moment was lost: Mercury screwed his neck and haled him to the lower regions, to that bourne "from which they say no traveller returns." As they passed downwards along the Sacred Way, Mercury asked what was that great concourse of men? could it be Claudius' funeral? It was certainly a most gorgeous spectacle, got up regardless of expense, clear it was that a god was being borne to the grave: tootling of flutes, roaring of horns, an immense brass band of all sorts, such a din that even Claudius could hear it. Joy and rejoicing on every side, the Roman people walking about like free men. Agatho and a few pettifoggers were weeping for grief, and for once in a way they meant it. The Barristers were crawling out of their dark corners, pale and thin, with hardly a breath in their bodies, as though just coming to life again. One of them when he saw the pettifoggers putting their heads together, and lamenting their sad lot, up comes he and says: "Did not I tell you the Saturnalia could not last for ever?"

When Claudius saw his own funeral train, he understood that he was dead. For they were chanting his dirge in anapaests, with much mopping and mouthing:

> Pour forth your laments, your sorrow declare,
> Let the sounds of grief rise high in the air:
> For he that is dead had a wit most keen,
> Was bravest of all that on earth have been.
> Racehorses are nothing to his swift feet:
> Rebellious Parthians he did defeat;
> Swift after the Persians his light shafts go:
> For he well knew how to fit arrow to bow.
> Swiftly the striped barbarians fled:
> With one little wound he shot them dead.
> And the Britons beyond in their unknown seas,
> Blue-shielded Brigantians too, all these
> He chained by the neck as the Romans' slaves.
> He spake, and the Ocean with trembling waves
> Accepted the axe of the Roman law.
> O weep for the man! This world never saw
> One quicker a troublesome suit to decide,
> When only one part of the case had been tried
> (He could do it indeed and not hear either side).
> Who'll now sit in judgment the whole year round?
> Now he that is judge of the shades underground,
> Once ruler of fivescore cities in Crete,
> Must yield to his better and take a back seat.
> Mourn, mourn, pettifoggers, ye venal crew,
> And you, minor poets, woe, woe is to you!
> And you above all, who get rich quick
> By the rattle of dice and the three card trick.

Claudius was charmed to hear his own praises sung, and would have stayed longer to see the show. But the Talthybius of the gods laid a hand on him, and led him across the Campus Martius, first wrapping his head up close that no one might know him, until betwixt Tiber and the Subway he went down to the lower regions. His freedman Narcissus had gone down before him by a short cut, ready to welcome his master. Out he comes to meet him, smooth and shining (he had just left the bath), and says he: "What make the gods among mortals?" "Look alive," says Mercury, "go and tell them we are coming." Away he flew, quicker than tongue can tell. It is easy going by that road, all down hill. So although he had a touch of the gout, in a trice they were come to Dis's door. There lay Cerberus, or, as Horace puts it, the hundred-headed monster. Claudius was a trifle perturbed (it was a little white bitch he used to keep for a pet) when he spied this black shag-haired hound, not at all the kind of thing you could wish to meet in the dark. In a loud voice he cried, "Claudius is coming!" All marched before him singing, "The lost is found, O let us rejoice together!" Here were found C. Silius consul elect, Juncus the ex-praetor, Sextus Traulus, M. Helvius, Trogus, Cotta, Vettius Valens, Fabius, Roman Knights whom Narcissus had ordered for execution. In the midst of this chanting company was Mnester the mime, whom Claudius for honour's sake had made shorter by a head. The news was soon blown about that Claudius had come: to Messalina they throng: first his freedmen, Polybius, Myron, Harpocras, Amphaeus, Pheronactus, all sent before him by Claudius that he might not be unattended anywhere; next two prefects, Justus Catonius and Rufrius Pollio; then his friends, Saturninus Lusius and Pedo Pompeius and Lupus and Celer Asinius, these of consular rank; last came his brother's daughter, his sister's daughter, sons-in-law, fathers and mothers-in-law, the whole family in fact. In a body they came to meet Claudius; and when Claudius saw them, he exclaimed, "Friends everywhere, on my word! How came you all here?" To this Pedo Pompeius answered, "What, cruel man? How came we here? Who but you sent us, you, the murderer of all the friends that you ever had? To court with you! I'll show you where their lordships sit."

Pedo brings him before the judgment seat of Aeacus, who was holding court under the Lex Cornelia to try cases of murder and assassination. Pedo requests the judge to take the prisoner's name, and produces a summons with this charge: Senators killed, 35; Roman Knights, 221; others as the sands of the sea-shore for multitude. Claudius finds no counsel. At length out steps P. Petronius, an old chum of his, a finished scholar in the Claudian tongue, and claims a remand. Not granted. Pedo Pompeius prosecutes amid loud applause. The counsel for the defense tries to reply; but Aeacus, who is the soul of justice, will not have it. Aeacus hears the case against Claudius, refuses to hear the other side and passes sentence against him, quoting the line:

As he did, so be he done by, this is justice undefiled.

A great silence fell. Not a soul but was stupefied at this new way of managing matters; they had never known anything like it before. It was no new thing to Claudius, yet he thought it unfair. There was a long discussion as to the punishment he ought to endure. Some said that Sisyphus had done his job of porterage long enough; Tantalus would be dying of thirst, if he were not relieved; the drag must be put at last on wretched Ixion's wheel. But it was determined not to let off any of the old stagers, lest Claudius should dare to hope for any such relief. It was agreed that some new punishment must be devised: they must devise some new task, something senseless, to suggest some craving without result. Then Aeacus decreed he should rattle dice for ever in a box with holes in the bottom. At once the poor wretch began his fruitless task of hunting for the dice, which for ever slipped from his fingers.

> For when he rattled with the box, and thought he now had got 'em,
> The little cubes would vanish thro' the perforated bottom.
> Then he would pick 'em up again, and once more set a-trying:
> The dice but served him the same trick: away they went a-flying.
> So still he tries, and still he fails; still searching long he lingers;
> And every time the tricksy things go slipping thro' his fingers.
> Just so when Sisyphus at last gets there with his boulder,
> He finds the labour all in vain—it rolls down off his shoulder.

All on a sudden who should turn up but Caligula, and claims the man for a slave: brings witnesses, who said they had seen him being flogged, caned, fisticuffed by him. He is handed over to Caligula, and Caligula makes him a present to Aeacus. Aeacus delivers him to his freedman Menander, to be his law-clerk.

Lucan: *Pharsalia*

The emperor Nero prided himself upon his artistic accomplishments. Poetry, singing, lyre-playing, and composition were all part of his repertory. Nero's reign (54–68 A.D.),
or at least the early part of it, provided a congenial atmosphere for Roman literature and produced figures like
Petronius, Seneca, and Lucan. Young Marcus Annaeus Lu-
canus (39–65 A.D.) was the nephew of Seneca and was brought
to the attention of the court by his uncle. Lucan's one
surviving work is his major production, the *Pharsalia,* an
historical epic poem which recounts the final struggle of
Caesar and Pompey, the death-throes of the Roman Republic. The work leaves no doubt as to Lucan's sympathies.
They lay with the Republic and its champions, an era
forgotten and crushed by the tyranny under which Lucan
himself lived. To be sure, the opening portions of the
Pharsalia present an invocation to the emperor, addressing
him with gross adulation. That was good etiquette and prudent. More important, however, is the character of the poem
itself. The civil war is not depicted as a necessary and
fruitful event which produced the glory of empire and the
imperial line of the Julio-Claudians. On the contrary, it
is the tragic struggle which brought to an untimely end the
Republic for which Lucan unashamedly mourns. Julius
Caesar, ancestor of the Julio-Claudian dynasty, is the blood-
thirsty warrior who relishes the destruction of the aristocracy; Pompey is the saddened victim who observed the Republic's fall. But Lucan's most fervent admiration goes out
to Cato, the symbol of the Republic, who preferred death
to subservience. The poet overtly resurrects the past to denounce the slavery under which his fellow men are compelled to live. As might be expected, Lucan suffered for his
pains. In 65 A.D. Nero ordered the execution of Lucan,
Seneca, and Petronius.

The following selections are from Lucan, *Pharsalia,* Book VII;
Book IX; trans. Robert Graves in *Lucan, Pharsalia* (Baltimore:

Penguin Books, Inc., 1957), 165–69, 210–12. Reprinted by permission of Penguin Books Ltd.

Panic spread, and Caesar's prospects visibly brightened. Pompey's centre, the strongest part of his army, now became involved; and the confused fighting which had been taking place in other quarters was concentrated here in a bitter engagement. The Caesareans had met worthy opponents at last: their own brothers and fathers, not foreign auxiliaries from distant kingdoms. This phase of the battle epitomised the evil fury sponsored by Caesar. I would rather not write about it; I refuse to acquaint posterity with the full horrors unchained by this civil war. Let my tears and complaints perish without record: I cannot bring myself to describe a clash between Roman legions. Caesar could be seen rushing from point to point, whipping up the frenzy which already possessed his men and inciting them to yet more desperate acts of wickedness. His eye was quick to notice which men had reddened their swords to the hilt, and which only to the point; which were merely obeying the order to fight and holding their weapons irresolutely, and which were enjoying the work so much that they never blanched at the murder of their fellow-citizens. He also stooped over the sprawled corpses and, if he found one of his men bleeding to death, staunched the flow by the pressure of his own fingers.

Caesar's progress resembled that of Bellona, Goddess of War, when she brandishes her bloody scourge; or Mars when he inspires the Bistonians of Thrace by lashing on his chariot horses—the same team which Athene once terrified by displaying her Aegis. Wherever he moved, a dark cloud of crime and slaughter accompanied him, and a concerted groan was heard, mixed with the clang of men's breastplates as they struck the ground, and of swords being shattered against swords. He was always there to hand his men new swords or weapons salvaged from the field: "Hack at their faces!" he shouted. He led the front ranks to the attack in person, but then took a javelin and slipped back to the rear where he beat malingerers forward with the butt end. "Never mind the private soldiers," he cried. "Kill the Senators!" For Caesar had his finger on the pulse of free Rome, now making her last stand on earth; he knew exactly how the blood flowed in her veins, and where she was most vulnerable. His men obeyed this new order and began hacking down all senators and knights: members of the Lepidan, Metellan, Corvinian, and Torquatan families, who had often commanded Roman armies and were the most distinguished men in the state, Pompey alone excepted.

But what was Brutus doing on this occasion, sword in hand and disguised as a private soldier—Brutus, glory of Rome, last survivor of a house famous in our history? He was rashly trying to cut his way through the enemy ranks and kill Caesar; careless of his life, but doomed to die later at Philippi in another battle as decisive as that of Pharsalus. Brutus's attempt proved idle, because Caesar had not yet risen above the decent limit of human greatness by tyrannizing over a prostrate world, and had not yet therefore earned the right to be assassinated. He would continue to live until Brutus won immortal fame by stabbing him with a dagger.

The flower of our nobility perished in that battle; a mound of patrician corpses afterwards found lying there contained not one plebeian. One death must be noted for attention: that of Domitius Ahenobarbus whom fate had led from defeat to defeat; whenever Pompey lost a battle he was always present—yet he died free. He fell cheerfully, wounded in a thousand places, and glad to escape the shame of being pardoned by Caesar a second time. Caesar found him weltering in his blood and remarked ironically: "Ah, it is you, Domitius, the man whom the Senate chose as Governor-General of Gaul instead of me! Are you deserting the Pompeian cause and retiring from the war?" The dying Domitius just managed to gasp out:

Caesar, you do not realize what a fearful price you will have to pay for your treason. And you are still no match for your son in law; you cannot yet count on victory. I go freely and happily to join the ghosts beside the river Styx, in the resolute hope that you will be crushed in battle and forced to indemnify Pompey and myself for the great mischief you have done us.

Then the darkness of death closed his eyes.

It would be wrong to pick on any further victims, among all these thousands, for particular lament, or to describe individual deaths—telling who was stabbed in the belly; whose intestines burst out and dangled to the ground where he trod on them; who faced the enemy and died with a sword piercing his throat

. . . Some wounded men collapsed; some continued to stand up-right, though their arms were lopped off; others had their breasts transfixed by a javelin, or were pinned to the earth with a spear-thrust. Often the blood spouted like a fountain and wetted the enemy's arms. One man drove his sword through his own brother's breast and, having decapitated him, threw away the head to avoid the disgrace of despoiling a near relative's corpse. Another mutilated his father's face, in a furious attempt to convince those who saw him that he had not committed parricide. No, this is hardly an occasion for mourning the fate of individuals. Pharsalus differed from all other Roman defeats in so much as whole armies died there—the allied forces of Greece, Pontus, and Assyria—and yet the torrent of Roman blood was enough to sweep theirs from the field. The world suffered an irreparable disaster, because what we lost at Pharsalus was more than life and property; Ro-man liberty lay prostrate and Caesar's swords sufficed thereafter to cow generation after generation. But do we great-grandchildren of the combatants really deserve to be born slaves? Are we cow-ards that we fear to die? No, this is a punishment for our fathers' fears: Fortune who gave us tyranny should have also given us a chance to take the field against our tyrants.

Though Pompey understood that the Gods had deserted Rome and himself, even a beaten army was not too terrible a sight to make him despair of final success. He stood on a knoll above the plain from which, now that the fighting was over, he could see corpses scattered everywhere and estimate the full extent of the losses. While feeling as if he were bleeding to death, he did not do what other ruined commanders have done in similar circum-stances: rejoice to drag the entire world down with him. He persuaded himself that the Gods were worth invoking, and con-sidered how to win their favour, despite the present calamity, consoling himself with the hope that the greater part of the Roman army might be rescued from destruction. "Gods of Heaven!" he prayed.

Hold your hands! Spare what yet remains of the world! Rome may still survive, even though I am doomed. Do you wish to chastise me still further? Then I have a wife and two sons left as hostages in Fortune's hands. Tell me: if I and they are destroyed, will that put an end to the Civil War? Will that sacrifice content you, or is it

fortune's whim to mangle and ruin the entire human race? I will-
ingly yield her all that remains mine.

Then he rounded up his dwindling army and had the retreat
blown, to prevent them from throwing away their lives in a now
hopeless cause. He did not, of course, shrink from offering his
throat or breast to the enemy swordsmen; but feared that, if he
did so, his men would continue to stand their ground and allow
themselves to be slaughtered in heaps above his corpse. Or perhaps he wished to die where Caesar would not be there to see?
If so, it was a vain hope: if Caesar chose to demand Pompey's
severed head, no land would grudge it him. And Pompey had
another reason for flight: the beloved face of his wife, without
whom he could not die, because she was a part of him.

He spurred his horse from the field, fearless of the javelins
flying behind him, and moved dauntlessly to his doom. He neither
groaned nor wept, but looked serenely on the plain of Pharsalus,
displaying the dignified sorrow which one might have expected
from so great a man when faced by the misfortunes of Rome.
Victory had never elated him, nor had defeat ever depressed him;
and faithless Fortune who owned him her superior in the time
of his three Triumphs, found that he was her superior still. After
surrendering the heavy burden entrusted to him by Fate, he rode
off with a light heart; and now found leisure to dwell upon the
happy past and, since hope was vanished beyond recall, dwell
contentedly upon what he once had been. How right to quit the
stricken field and make the Gods witnesses that any soldiers who
cared to fight on were no longer dying for his sake!

As in the lamentable battles of Thapsus and Munda, as in the
slaughter on the banks of the Nile, so at Pharsalus, when Pompey
had fled, the struggle ceased to be between those who loved him
and those who loved fighting. Rather, it was the struggle, which
continues to-day, between Freedom and Caesardom; and the senators proved by their willingness to die that a constitutional, not
a personal, dispute underlay it.

Pompey must, I think, have felt relieved to ride off, without
staying to watch the final scene of the disaster; but as he glanced
back at the fountains of blood that spurted from the dying and
darkened the streams of the Enipeus, he might well have pitied
Caesar. How would Caesar feel when he entered Rome again

after such a victory? Whatever sufferings might lie ahead of
Pompey, as a solitary exile in strange lands or as a prisoner of
King Ptolemy, his former patrons the Olympian Gods and Fortune
could give him one certain consolation: that victory would have
been worse than defeat. And the universal grief, mourning and
tears for Pompey's fall were inappropriate; he deserved as much
adoration in his present abasement as in his past Triumphs.
Calmly and with none of the self-abasement that suppliants affect,
he considered all the cities which he had taken, all the kingdoms
which he had bestowed on his allies in Egypt and Africa; and
chose from among them one where he might end his life.

*   *   *

Ammon's shrine was besieged that day by emissaries of Eastern
powers, all asking for advice about the future; but as soon as a
Roman general approached everyone politely made way for him.
Cato's officers pressed him to test and report on the veracity of
this Oracle, which had been famous throughout Africa for many
centuries. Labienus was particularly urgent. He told Cato:

> It so happens that our march has taken us to the Oracle of this
> mighty god; let us use his divine guidance for our passage along
> the Gulf of Sirte and discover how this war is fated to end. I cannot
> think of any man for whom Heaven would be readier to reveal the
> hidden truth than your pure and virtuous self. It is clear that you
> have always lived in accordance with divine principle, and are a
> follower of God. And, look, here is an opportunity for a conference
> with Juppiter Ammon himself. Why not ask him what the fate
> of that criminal Caesar will be and what will happen to Rome?
> Why not find out whether constitutional liberty will be restored or
> whether we are fighting this war in vain? Take a deep breath and
> utter the holy prayer required. As an austere lover of virtue, you
> should at least ask Ammon in what virtue consists, and demand a
> directive for the future.

But Cato carried a god in his own heart and replied in words
worthy of the Oracle itself. "Come, Labienus!" he said.

> Precisely what question do you want me to put? Whether I should
> prefer to die in battle, still a free man, or live under tyranny?
> Or whether it does not matter if life be long or short? Or whether
> honest men can be harmed by the violence of fortune? Or whether

it is enough to be virtuous without troubling to be successful? I could answer each of these questions, and need no oracle to confirm my opinion. Men cannot, logically, be separated from gods, because whatever we do has been predestined. And there is no necessity for the Gods to give responses; the author of the Universe told us at our birth, once and for all, as much as we are allowed to know. Do you really think that he has chosen this desert for his shrine in order to limit the number of visitants and so, as it were, bury the divine truth in drifting sand? What other dwelling place has God but earth, sea, air, and righteous hearts? Why should we need more gods than God? Whatever we see and do must be manifestations of God. Whoever feels anxiety about the future may pray for prophecies; but I can tell exactly where my duty lies, and not because any oracle has given me advice, but because I know that I must die. One may be brave or one may be cowardly; nevertheless, death is certain. That was what God told me at birth, and it is enough for me.

So saying, Cato moved away from the shrine, without either testing the Oracle or disparaging it, and left the orientals to pay their devotions in peace. Then on he went at the head of his column, not riding in a litter or a chariot, as some generals do, but on foot, javelin in hand; and made his panting troops endure their ordeal by example, rather than compulsion. He slept little and was always the last to drink: whenever after a long day's march, a spring had been discovered and a queue formed at the drinking hole, Cato waited for the humblest camp-follower to quench his thirst. It occurs to me that if fame be the reward of true and unadorned virtue, whether successful or not, then we should call most of our ancestors less famous than fortunate. None of them, by the slaughter of foreign armies, ever won such fame as Cato. Myself, I should much prefer to be remembered as a Cato who led his army around the Gulf of Sirte and through distant parts of Libya, than as a Pompey who celebrated three Triumphs at Rome; or as a Marius who defeated Jugurtha and then had him strangled in prison. Cato was a true father of his country, and far worthier than others who have since been granted this title, to have altars raised in his memory. One day when we are finally freed from slavery, if that ever happens, Cato will be deified; and Rome will then have a god by whose name it need not be ashamed to swear.

Part Four

THE GROWTH OF MONARCHY

The eighteenth-century British historian Edward Gibbon regarded the "Age of the Antonines" as the happiest era of human history. The period referred to comprised the years 96–180 A.D. Rome had a fortunate succession of competent rulers—from Nerva and Trajan to Marcus Aurelius—whom moderns customarily describe as "the good emperors." Gibbon's favorable judgment has frequently been echoed by his successors and can be read also in the ancient sources. The emperors of the second century A.D. rose considerably in stature by comparison with what had gone before. When the Julio-Claudian line perished with the suicide of Nero, Rome was engulfed again in civil war, this time involving provincial armies and foreign revolts in Gaul and Germany. After order was restored, a new dynasty, the house of the Flavians, ruled Rome for a quarter of a century. Even the hated Julio-Claudians had not matched the horrors and tyranny which tradition ascribes to the last of the Flavians, Domitian. Naked autocracy led to the decimation of the senatorial class. Domitian claimed divinity as well as absolute authority; the reign ended, inevitably, in assassination. The men who sat on the throne during the following century consciously contrasted their regimes with the Domitianic terror. Consequently, the "good emperors" have received a good press. One must bear in mind that the imperial images are largely the creation of Rome's articulate and intellectual classes. The tradition that judges the emperors is drawn from the aristocracy and focuses upon the treatment of the aristocracy. By that standard, the rulers from Nerva to Marcus Aurelius rate high. They were careful not to offend their peers and not to flaunt their authority.

As a result, the institution of monarchy was no longer challenged. The second century called forth no tracts which sought to resurrect the spirit of the Republic or undermine the ruler's position. Political theory developed a new line: the ideal of a constitutional monarch. The emperor was the indispensable mainstay of government. But he was expected to operate in accordance with the laws, to collaborate with the senate, and to serve as shepherd of his people. The second-century rulers appeared to fit the bill and their panegyrists responded accordingly. Pliny's address to the Emperor Trajan in 100 A.D. expresses the doctrine most clearly. His oration evinces unbounded faith in the virtue and benevolence of the monarch who adheres to the constitution and reflects divine justice. Marcus Aurelius, later in the century, represented the closest approximation to the ideal. The philosopher-emperor applied Stoic principles to the duties of the imperial office. And historians too could reflect the era. Dio Cassius grew to maturity in the reign of Marcus Aurelius. He expounded a classic justification for monarchy: order, continuity, and the stable management of a vast empire.

One will not find in the second century critics of monarchy as an institution. But some intellectuals who suffered under the Domitianic terror and survived into the new era could see with broader perspective. The historian Tacitus acknowledged the necessity and advantages of one-man rule, but he was not blind to its costs. The ancient and vigorous tradition of Roman oratory had flourished in a chaotic but free society. There was no room for it in a system which required conformity. Similarly, the satirist Juvenal was prudent enough to fire his shafts not at the "good emperors" under whom he published, but at Domitian who was dead and gone. A perceptive reader, however, would note that Juvenal's debunking of the imperial council could apply with equal force to any ruler. Discontent, even in the age of the Antonines, was not altogether stilled.

Pliny: *Panegyric to Trajan*

Trajan ascended the throne of Rome in 98 A.D. after the brief reign of Nerva. It was the new monarch's concern to contrast his qualities and regime sharply with the grim years of Domitian that had preceded. A proper attitude toward the intellectual and senatorial classes was the best vehicle. Not that senators possessed any more power under Trajan. But the emperor prudently allowed them to believe they did. The services of Gaius Plinius Secundus (ca. 61–113 A.D.) proved most useful. Pliny was a cultured aristocrat, a philanthropist, orator, and center of a large intellectual circle. The information contained in his corpus of letters provides our fullest and most important evidence for the Trajanic years. In the latter part of his life Pliny was the emperor's personal agent, charged with reorganizing the finances of the province Bithynia. But his presence in Rome early in the reign was equally valuable. Trajan appointed Pliny to the consulship in 100 A.D. and the latter responded by delivering his *Panegyricus* to the emperor. The speech outlined the virtues and benefits of Trajan's reign. The monarch exemplifies a new monarchic ideal. Domitian's dismal days are forever a thing of the past. Trajan places himself under the aegis of law, promotes collaboration with his peers, and exercises judgment in accordance with divine justice. Most important, the emperor is simply a first among equals. He shuns the trappings and aura of divinity. He regards himself the equal of his fellow-citizens. The purpose of the monarch is not to lord it over his subjects, but to govern in their interests and for their advantage. This image of the ideal ruler perpetuated itself through the Antonine age.

The following selections are from Pliny, *Panegyricus*, Secs. 1–2, 21, 24, 65–68, 80 (with omissions) trans. by the editor.

Members of the senate, our ancestors instituted a wise and salutary practice in beginning speeches as well as actions with prayers to the gods; because proper form and good prospects in human endeavor can come only with the aid, the counsel, and the dignity of the immortal gods. Who can better take up and observe such a practice than a consul, and what occasion is more propitious than one in which we are bidden by order of the senate and in the name of the state to express gratitude to the best of emperors? What gift of the gods is more precious or beautiful than an emperor who is chaste, pious, and godlike? And if it had hitherto been uncertain whether our earthly rulers were given us by chance or by design, it should now be clear that this emperor of ours is divinely appointed. . . . It is all the more suitable and pious, therefore, that I invoke you, O kindest Jupiter, once founder, now preserver of our empire, to see to it that my oration be worthy of a consul, of this senate, and of this emperor; that freedom, sincerity, and truth inform all my words; and that my expression of gratitude be as divorced from flattery as it is from constraint. . . .

I do not flatter him as if he were a god or a divine being. For I speak not of a tyrant, but of a citizen, not of a master, but of a parent. He stands out and excels all the more because he regards himself as one of us and is no less mindful of the fact that he is both a man and a ruler of men. Let us therefore ponder our good fortune, let us prove ourselves worthy of his service, and let us consider repeatedly whether we owe greater obeisance to emperors who rejoice in our slavery than to those who rejoice in our freedom.

*   *   *

With virtues of such quality and quantity did you not deserve some new titles and new honors? Yet you declined even the title of "father of your country." How lengthy a struggle we had to overcome your modesty! How long it was before we finally prevailed! That title which others assumed on the first day of their reign, as they did those of *imperator* and *Caesar,* you held at arms' length, until at last, despite your most modest estimate of your benefactions, you acknowledged its appropriateness. Of you alone it could be said that you *were* father of your country before you became "father of your country." You were such in our hearts and in our judgment; and lack of the title was of no importance except that to public piety it seemed ingratitude to

call you emperor and Caesar when it found in you a father. With
what bounty and what kindness you bore that name! You live
with your fellow citizens as a father does with his children. In
moving from private citizen to emperor you rediscovered them
and they you. In your eyes, we are the same as before, and you
the same as before. You are on a par with everyone, greater only
in that you are better.

*　　　　*　　　　*

Each day you grow more admirable and more perfect. You became what other emperors only promised to be. You alone secure
advantage and improvement with the passage of time. You have
united and combined the most diverse qualities: modesty in under-
taking your task, assurance in carrying it out. . . . The kindliness
of your visage marks the emperor as it did the private citizen.
You travel by foot, as you did before; you rejoice in your labor,
as you did before. Good fortune, which has changed everything
around you, has changed you not at all. When the emperor appears in public every man is free to stop him, to address him, to
accompany him, or to pass him by. . . . Whoever approaches
you remains at your side, and respect—not your arrogance—puts
an end to his conversation. We are governed by you and submit
to you, but only as we submit to the laws. They too govern our
desires and passions, that we may live with and among ourselves.
Your quality and excellence are like honor and power: superior
to men but the product of men. Emperors before you, either
out of scorn for us or a certain fear of equality, lost the use of
their feet. The shoulders and necks of slaves bore them above us;
fame, glory, respect of citizens, and freedom bear you above emperors themselves. That common earth which mingles the traces
of emperor and citizens alike raises you to the stars.

*　　　　*　　　　*

You have subjected yourself to the laws, Caesar, láws which
no one ever meant for an emperor. But you want no more rights
for yourself than we enjoy; consequently we seek all the more
for you. What I now hear for the first time, what I now learn for
the first time is not "emperor above the laws," but "laws above
the emperor"; and the same limitations apply to Caesar when
consul as to all others. He swears loyalty to the laws with the gods

in attendance (for whom would the gods be more likely to attend than Caesar?); he swears loyalty in the company of those who utter the same oath, aware that no one must be more faithful to his vow than he for whom its fulfillment is most important. Upon resigning the consulship you took an oath that you had done nothing contrary to the laws. It was impressive when you promised it; even more impressive when you fulfilled it. . . ,

On the very first day of your consulship you entered the senate house and urged us, singly and as a group, to resume our freedom, to collaborate with you in the common burden of empire, to rise and guard the interests of state. All your predecessors had said the same; none, before you, was believed. The shipwreck of so many men was before our eyes, men carried along by a deceptive tranquillity and then wrecked by sudden storm. For what sea is as faithless as the blandishments of emperors so given to fickleness and hypocrisy that it would be easier to protect oneself against their anger than against their favor? But you we follow, swiftly and confidently, wherever you summon. You order us to be free; we will be; you order us to express what we feel; we will do so. We have hesitated until now, not out of cowardice or idleness; terror, fear, and that wretched prudence learned in danger warned us to avert our eyes, our ears, and our minds from the republic (which was not altogether a republic). But now, trusting and leaning on your strong right arm and your promises, we unseal our lips, closed for so long in servitude, and loosen our tongues, paralyzed by so many evils. You want us to be as you order. In your exhortations there is nothing counterfeit, nothing fraudulent, nothing which appears to deceive the believer at the peril of the deceiver. The emperor who does not mislead will not be misled.

Here is the image of the father of our state as I seem to perceive it, both from his speech and from his delivery. What authority in his ideas, what unalloyed candor in his words, what conviction in his voice, what firmness in his expression, what sincerity in his eyes, appearance, gestures, in fact his whole body! He will always hold to what he advised, and he will know that whenever we exercise the liberty which he granted we are obeying his counsel. There is no fear that he will think us reckless if we take full advantage of the security of this age, for he remembers how differently we behaved under an evil emperor. It is our practice to pledge ourselves for the eternity of the empire and the security of its emperors, or rather for the security of the emperors and, through them, for the eternity of the empire. But it is worth noting how the words read for this emperor of ours: "if he rules the state well and in the interests of all." These are pledges always worth repeating and fulfilling. On your authority, Caesar, the state has contracted with the gods for your safety and well-being as long as you assure the same for all others. . . . Others hope and aim to outlive the state; for you personal security itself is unthinkable unless combined with the security of the state. You allow nothing to be requested on your behalf unless it is of benefit to those who made the request. . . . It is with a pure conscience, Caesar, that you have contracted with the gods that they protect you if you deserve it, for you are aware that no one knows better than the gods how deserving you are. . . .

You reap the most glorious fruit, Caesar, that of your salvation, from the consent of the gods. For when you announce that the gods will protect you only so long as you govern the state well and in the interests of all, you are assured of the beneficence of your rule while they continue to protect you. So you enjoy in security and happiness the day which tortured other emperors with worry and fear as they awaited in stupefied suspense, unsure of our loyalty, the announcements of public servitude. And if, by chance, floods, snow, or winds delayed those messages, the emperors immediately feared that they would get what they deserved. The terror is always the same: for an evil emperor fears as his successor anyone who is more worthy than he; and if no one is more worthy, he fears everyone. In your case, however, no hindrance or delay of messages and announcements impairs your security. You know that pledges are taken everywhere in your behalf, for you have pledged yourself for everyone. . . . Our love for you is consonant with your merits; but that love is felt not so much on your behalf as on our own. May the day never dawn when our vows for you, Caesar, are inspired by mere loyalty rather than by our own advantage.

*   *   *

In all your judicial decisions, how mild is your severity, how firm your clemency! You do not sit in judgment for the purpose of filling your treasury; nor do you seek any reward other than that of having judged properly. Litigants stand before you con-

cerned not for their pocketbooks but for your good opinion, and
they fear not so much what you think of their case, but what you
think of their conduct. These are concerns truly of a prince, indeed
of a god, to reconcile rival states, to calm turbulent peoples by
reason more than by power, to correct the inequities of magistrates, to annul everything which was done improperly, and finally,
in the manner of the swiftest star, to investigate everything, to
hear everything, and, like a divine being, wherever you are invoked, to be immediately present and helpful. It is in this way, I
believe, that the father of the world rules with his nod whenever
he casts his eyes upon earth and deigns to reckon human affairs
among the concerns of the divine. He is now free and released
from this concern in heaven, for he has sent us you to serve as
his agent among men. You fulfill that function and are worthy of
his charge, for each of your days is spent in pursuit of our greatest good and of your everlasting glory.

Marcus Aurelius: Meditations

The principles enunciated by Pliny were no better exemplified than in the reign of Marcus Aurelius (161–180
A.D.). Marcus was born Marcus Annius Verus in 121 A.D.,
first caught the eye of the emperor Hadrian, and was nur-
tured for empire under the reign of Antoninus Pius. He
took the throne at the age of forty, equipped with long
training, a fine mind, and a powerful sense of duty. Few
men have so captured the imagination of students and
scholars. Matthew Arnold called him "perhaps the most
beautiful figure in history." Marcus' reign was difficult and
grim. Rome suffered through a grievous plague, military
revolt in the east, and almost incessant Germanic incur-
sions on the Danube. Marcus spent the last years of his
life on the Danube, defending the frontiers, and fighting
off the crippling effects of disease. Stoic philosophy was a
comfort and a refuge. The Meditations were composed in
those latter years on the frontiers. They do not form a systematic treatise but a series of random jottings. It has been

rightly said that we do not so much read the *Meditations* as overhear them. They possess the fresh quality of authenticity, rather than artificial elaboration. Devotion to duty is a theme stressed throughout. Humility is the hallmark of the emperor, and a recognition of the transitoriness of glory. The ruler's aim is to curb his ambitions and meet his obligations. Stoic principles brought belief in a commonwealth of men. It is a remarkable document. No less remarkable is the fact that Marcus lived it as well as he wrote it. But one cannot escape the dominant note of melancholy. Marcus' thoughts do not represent affirmation so much as resignation. The man who most closely approximated the ideal ruler did not enjoy his role.

The following selections are from Marcus Aurelius, *Meditations*, Book VI, Sec. 30; Book IX, Secs. 1–42, trans. Maxwell Staniforth in *Marcus Aurelius, Meditations* (Baltimore: Penguin Books, Inc., 1964), 97–98, 137–49. Reprinted by permission of Penguin Books Ltd.

30. Be careful not to affect the monarch too much, or to be too deeply dyed with the purple; for this can well happen. Keep yourself simple, good, pure, serious, and unassuming; the friend of justice and godliness; kindly, affectionate, and resolute in your devotion to duty. Strive your hardest to be always such a man as Philosophy would have you to be. Reverence the gods, succour your fellow-mortals. Life is short, and this earthly existence has but a single fruit to yield—holiness within, and selfless action without. Be in all things Antoninus's disciple; remember his insistence on the control of conduct by reason, his calm composure on all occasions, and his own holiness; the serenity of his look and the sweetness of his manner; his scorn of notoriety, and his zeal for the mastery of facts; how he would never dismiss a subject until he had looked thoroughly into it and understood it clearly; how he would suffer unjust criticisms without replying in kind; how he was never hasty, and no friend to tale-bearers; shrewd in his judgements of men and manners, yet never censorious; wholly free from nervousness, suspicion, and oversubtlety; how easily satisfied he was in such matters as lodging, bed, dress, meals, and service; how industrious, and how patient; how, thanks to his frugal diet, he could remain at work from morning till night with-

out even attending to the calls of nature until his customary hour;
how firm and constant he was in his friendships, tolerating the
most outspoken opposition to his own opinions, and welcoming
any suggested amendments; what reverence, untainted by the
smallest trace of superstition, he showed to the gods. Remember
all this, so that when your own last hour comes your conscience
may be as clear as his.

*   *   *

1. Injustice is a sin. Nature has constituted rational beings for
their own mutual benefit, each to help his fellows according to
their worth, and in no wise to do them hurt; and to contravene her
will is plainly to sin against this eldest of all the deities. Untruth-
fulness, too, is a sin, and against the same goddess. For Nature is
the nature of Existence itself; and existence connotes the kinship
of all created beings. Truth is but another name for this Nature,
the original creator of all true things. So, where a wilful lie is a
sin because the deception is an act of injustice, an involuntary lie
is also a sin because it is a discordant note in Nature's harmony,
and creates mutinous disorder in an orderly universe. For mutinous
indeed it is, when a man lets himself be carried, even involuntarily,
into a position contrary to truth; seeing that he has so neglected
the faculties Nature gave him that he is no longer able to distin-
guish the false from the true.

Again, it is a sin to pursue pleasure as a good and to avoid pain as
an evil. It is bound to result in complaints that Nature is unfair in
her rewarding of vice and virtue; since it is the bad who are so
often in enjoyment of pleasures and the means to obtain them,
while pains and events that occasion pains descend upon the heads
of the good. Besides, if a man is afraid of pain, he is afraid of
something happening which will be part of the appointed order
of things, and this is itself a sin; if he is bent on the pursuit of
pleasure, he will not stop at acts of injustice, which again is mani-
festly sinful. No; when Nature herself makes no distinction and if
she did, she would not have brought pains and pleasures into existence side by side—it behoves those who would follow in her foot-
steps to be like-minded and exhibit the same indifference. He
therefore who does not view with equal unconcern pain or pleasure, death or life, fame or dishonour—all of them employed by
Nature without any partiality—clearly commits a sin. And in say-

ing that nature employs them without partiality, I mean that every successive generation of created things equally passes through the same experiences in turn; for this is the outcome of the original impulse which in the beginning moved Providence—by taking certain germs of future existences, and endowing them with productive powers of self-realization, of mutation, and of succession—to progress from the inception of the universe to its present orderly system.

2. A man of finer feelings would have taken leave of the world before ever sampling its falsehood, double-dealing, luxury, and pride; but now that all these have been tasted to satiety, the next best course would be to end your life forthwith. Or are you really resolved to go on dwelling in the midst of iniquity and has experience not yet persuaded you to flee from the pestilence? For infection of the mind is a far more dangerous pestilence than any unwholesomeness or disorder in the atmosphere around us. Insofar as we are animals, the one attacks our lives; but as men, the other attacks our manhood.

3. Despise not death; smile, rather, at its coming; it is among the things that Nature wills. Like youth and age, like growth and maturity, like the advent of teeth, beard, and grey hairs, like begetting, pregnancy, and childbirth, like every other natural process that life's seasons bring us, so is our dissolution. Never, then, will a thinking man view death lightly, impatiently, or scornfully; he will wait for it as but one more of Nature's processes. Even as you await the baby's emergence from the womb of your wife, so await the hour when the little soul shall glide forth from its sheath.

But if your heart would have comfort of a simpler sort, then there is no better solace in the face of death than to think on the nature of the surroundings you are leaving, and the characters you will no longer have to mix with. Not that you must find these offensive; rather, your duty is to care for them and bear with them mildly; yet never forget that you are parting from men of far other principles than your own. One thing, if any, might have held you back and bound you to life; the chance of fellowship with kindred minds. But when you contemplate the weariness of an existence in company so discordant, you cry, "Come quickly, Death, lest I too become forgetful of myself."

4. The sinner sins against himself; the wrongdoer wrongs himself, becoming the worse by his own action.

5. A man does not sin by commission only, but often by omission.

6. Enough if your present opinion be grounded in conviction, your present action grounded in unselfishness, and your present disposition contented with whatever befalls you from without.

7. Erase fancy; curb impulse; quench desire; let sovereign reason have the mastery.

8. A single life-principle is divided amongst all irrational creatures, and a single mind-principle distributed among the rational; just as this one earth gives form to all things earthy, and just as all of us who have sight and breath see by the self-same light and breathe of the self-same air.

9. All things that share the same element tend to seek their own kind. Things earthy gravitate towards earth, things aqueous flow towards one another, things aerial likewise—whence the need for the barriers which keep them forcibly apart. The tendency of flames is to mount skyward, because of the elemental fire; even here below, they are so eager for the company of their own kind that any sort of material, if it be reasonably dry, will ignite with ease, since there is only a minority of its ingredients which is resistant to fire. In the same way, therefore, all portions of the universal Mind are drawn towards one another. More strongly, indeed; since, being higher in the scale of creation, their eagerness to blend and combine with their affinities is proportionately keener. This instinct for reunion shows itself in its first stage among the creatures without reason, when we see bees swarming, cattle herding, birds nesting in colonies, and couples mating; because in them soul has already emerged, and in such relatively higher forms of life as theirs the desire for union is found at a level of intensity which is not present in stones or sticks. When we come to beings with reason, there are political associations, comradeships, family life, public meetings, and in times of war treaties and armistices; and among the still higher orders, a measure of unity even exists between bodies far separated from one another—as for example with the stars. Thus ascent in the ranks of creation can induce fellow-feeling even where there is no proximity.

Yet now see what happens. It is we—we, intelligent beings—who alone have forgotten this mutual zeal for unity; among us alone the currents are not seen to converge. Nevertheless, though man may flee as he will, he is still caught and held fast; Nature is too strong for him. Observe with care, and you will see: you will sooner find a fragment of earth unrelated to the rest of earth than a man who is utterly without some link with his fellows.

10. Everything bears fruit; man, God, the whole universe, each in its proper season. No matter that the phrase is restricted in common use to vines and such like. Reason, too, yields fruit, both for itself and for the world; since from it comes a harvest of other good things, themselves all bearing the stamp of reason.

11. Teach them better, if you can; if not, remember that kindliness has been given you for moments like these. The gods themselves show kindness to such men; and at times, so indulgent are they, will even aid them in their endeavours to secure health, wealth, or reputation. This you too could do; who is there to hinder you?

12. Work yourself hard, but not as if you were being made a victim, and not with any desire for sympathy or admiration. Desire one thing alone: that your actions or inactions alike should be worthy of a reasoning citizen.

13. Today I have got myself out of all my perplexities; or rather, I have got the perplexities out of myself—for they were not without, but within; they lay in my own outlook.

14. Everything is banal in experience, fleeting in duration, sordid in content; in all respects the same today as generations now dead and buried have found it to be.

15. Facts stand wholly outside our gates; they are what they are, and no more; they know nothing about themselves, and they pass no judgement upon themselves. What is it, then, that pronounces the judgement? Our own guide and ruler, Reason.

16. A rational and social being is not affected in himself for either better or worse by his feelings, but by his will; just as his outward behaviour, good or bad, is the product of will, not of feelings.

17. For the thrown stone there is no more evil in falling than there is good in rising.

18. Penetrate into their inmost minds, and you will see what manner of critics you are afraid of, and how capable they are of criticizing themselves.

19. All things are in process of change. You yourself are cease-

lessly undergoing transformation, and the decay of some of your parts, and so is the whole universe.

20. Leave another's wrongdoing where it lies.

21. In the interruption of an activity, or the discontinuance and, as it were, death of an impulse, or an opinion, there is no evil. Look back at the phases of your own growth: childhood, boyhood, youth, age: each change itself a kind of death. Was this so frightening? Or take the lives you lived under your grandfather and then under your mother and then your father; trace the numerous differences and changes and discontinuances there were in those days, and ask yourself, "Were they so frightening?" No more so, then, is the cessation, the interruption, the change from life itself.

22. Your own mind, the Mind of the universe, your neighbour's mind—be prompt to explore them all. Your own, so that you may shape it to justice; the universe's, that you may recollect what it is you are a part of; your neighbour's, that you may understand whether it is informed by ignorance or knowledge, and also may recognize that it is kin to your own.

23. As a unit yourself, you help to complete the social whole; and similarly, therefore, your every action should help to complete the social life. Any action which is not related either directly or remotely to this social end disjoints that life, and destroys its unity. It is as much the act of a schismatic as when some citizen in a community does his utmost to dissociate himself from the general accord.

24. Childish squabbles, childish games, "petty breaths supporting corpses"—why, the ghosts in Homer have more evident reality!

25. First get at the nature and quality of the original cause, separate it from the material to which it has given shape, and study it; then determine the possible duration of its effects.

26. The woes you have had to bear are numberless because you were not content to let Reason, your guide and master, do its natural work. Come now, no more of this!

27. When those about you are venting their censure or malice upon you, or raising any other sort of injurious clamour, approach and penetrate into their souls, and see what manner of men they are. You will find little enough reason for all your painstaking efforts to win their good opinion. All the same, it still remains your duty to think kindly of them; for Nature has made them to be

your friends, and even the gods themselves lend them every sort of help, by dreams and by oracles, to gain the ends on which their hearts are set.

28. Upwards and downwards, from age to age, the cycles of the universe follow their unchanging round. It may be that the World-Mind wills each separate happening in succession; and if so, then accept the consequences. Or, it may be, there was but one primal act of will, of which all else is the sequel; every event being thus the germ of another. To put it another way, things are either isolated units, or they form one inseparable whole. If that whole be God, then all is well; but if aimless chance, at least you need not be aimless also.

Soon earth will cover us all. Then in time earth, too, will change; later, what issues from this change will itself in turn incessantly change, and so again will all that then takes its place, even unto the world's end. To let the mind dwell on these swiftly rolling billows of change and transformation is to know a contempt for all things mortal.

29. The primal Cause is like a river in flood; it bears everything along. How ignoble are the little men who play at politics and persuade themselves that they are acting in the true spirit of philosophy. Babes, incapable even of wiping their noses! What then, you who are a man? Why, do what nature is asking of you at this moment. Set about it as the opportunity offers, and no glancing around to see if you are observed. But do not expect Plato's ideal commonwealth; be satisfied if even a trifling endeavour comes off well, and count the result no mean success. For who can hope to alter men's convictions; and without change of conviction what can there be but grudging subjection and feigned assent? Oh yes; now go on and talk to me of Alexander, and Philip, and Demetrius of Phaleron. If those men did in truth understand the will of Nature and school themselves to follow it, that is their own affair. But if it was nothing more than a stage-role they were playing, no court has condemned me to imitate their example. Philosophy is a modest profession, all simplicity and plain dealing. Never try to seduce me into solemn pretentiousness.

30. Look down from above on the numberless herds of mankind, with their mysterious ceremonies, their divers voyagings in storm and calm, and all the chequered pattern of their comings and gatherings and goings. Go on to consider the life of bygone

generations; and then the life of all those who are yet to come; and even at the present day, the life of the hordes of far-off savages. In short, reflect what multitudes there are who are ignorant of your very name; how many more will have speedily forgotten it; how many, perhaps praising you now, who will soon enough be abusing you; and that therefore remembrance, glory, and all else together are things of no worth.

31. When beset from without by circumstance, be unperturbed; when prompted from within to action, be just and fair: in fine, let both will and deed issue in behaviour that is social and fulfils the law of your being.

32. Many of the anxieties that harass you are superfluous: being but creatures of your own fancy, you can rid yourself of them and expand into an ampler region, letting your thought sweep over the entire universe, contemplating the illimitable tracts of eternity, marking the swiftness of change in each created thing, and contrasting the brief span between birth and dissolution with the endless aeons that precede the one and the infinity that follows the other.

33. A little while, and all that is before your eyes now will have perished. Those who witness its passing will go the same road themselves before long; and then what will there be to choose between the oldest grandfather and the baby that died in its cradle?

34. Observe the instincts that guide these men; the ends they struggle for; the grounds on which they like and value things. In short, picture their souls laid bare. Yet they imagine their praises or censures have weight to help or hurt. What presumption!

35. Loss is nothing else but change, and change is Nature's delight. Ever since the world began, things have been ordered by her decree in the selfsame fashion as they are at this day, and as other similar things will be ordered to the end of time. How, then, can you say that it is all amiss, and ever will be so; that no power among all the gods in heaven can avail to mend it; and that the world lies condemned to a thraldom of ills without end?

36. The substance of us all is doomed to decay; the moisture and the clay, the bones, and the fetor. Our precious marble is but a callosity of the earth, our gold and silver her sediment; our raiment shreds of hair, our purple a fish's gore; and thus with all things else. So too is the very breath of our lives—ever passing as it does from this one to that.

37. Enough of this miserable way of life, these everlasting grumbles, these monkey antics. Why must you agitate yourself so? Nothing unprecedented is happening; so what is it that disturbs you? The form of it? Take a good look at it. The matter of it? Look well at that, too. Beyond form and matter, there is nothing more. Even at this late hour, set yourself to become a simpler and better man in the sight of the gods. For the mastering of that lesson, three years are as good as a hundred.

38. If he sinned, the harm is his own. Yet perhaps, after all, he did not.

39. Either things must have their origin in one single intelligent source, and all fall into place to compose, as it were, one single body—in which case no part ought to complain of what happens for the good of the whole—or else the world is nothing but atoms and their confused minglings and dispersions. So why be so harassed? Say to the Reason at your helm, "Come, are you dead and in decay? Is this some part you are playing? Have you sunk to the level of a beast of the field, grazing and herding with the rest?"

40. The gods either have power or they have not. If they have not, why pray to them? If they have, then instead of praying to be granted or spared such-and-such a thing, why not rather pray to be delivered from dreading it, or lusting for it, or grieving over it? Clearly, if they can help a man at all, they can help him in this way. You will say, perhaps, "But all that is something they have put in my own power." Then surely it were better to use your power and be a free man, than to hanker like a slave and a beggar for something that is not in your power. Besides, who told you the gods never lend their aid even towards things that do lie in our own power? Begin praying in this way, and you will see. Where another man prays "Grant that I may possess this woman," let your own prayer be, "Grant that I may not lust to possess her." Where he prays, "Grant me to be rid of such-and-such a one," you pray, "Take from me my desire to be rid of him." Where he begs, "Spare me the loss of my precious child," beg rather to be delivered from the terror of losing him. In short, give your petitions a turn in this direction, and see what comes.

41. "When I was sick," says Epicurus, "I never used to talk about my bodily ailments. I did not," he says, "discuss any topics of that kind with my visitors. I went on dealing with the principles of natural philosophy; and the point I particularly dwelt on

was how the mind, while having its part in all these commotions of the flesh, can still remain unruffled and pursue its own proper good. Nor," he adds, "did I give the doctors a chance to brag of their own triumphs; my life merely went on its normal way, smoothly and happily." In sickness, then, if you are sick, or in trouble of any other kind, be like Epicurus. Never let go your hold on philosophy for anything that may befall, and never take part in the nonsense that is talked by the ignorant and uninstructed (this is a maxim on which all schools agree). Concentrate wholly on the task before you, and on the instrument you possess for its accomplishment.

42. When you are outraged by somebody's impudence, ask yourself at once, "Can the world exist without impudent people?" It cannot; so do not ask for impossibilities. That man is simply one of the impudent whose existence is necessary to the world. Keep the same thought present, whenever you come across roguery, double-dealing or any other form of obliquity. You have only to remind yourself that the type is indispensable, and at once you will feel kindlier towards the individual. It is also helpful if you promptly recall what special quality Nature has given us to counter such particular faults. For there are antidotes with which she has provided us: gentleness to meet brutality, for example, and other correctives for other ills. Generally speaking, too, you have the opportunity of showing the culprit his blunder—for everyone who does wrong is failing of his proper objective, and is thereby a blunderer. Besides, what harm have you suffered? Nothing has been done by any of these victims of your irritation that could hurtfuly affect your own mind; and it is in the mind alone that anything evil or damaging to the self can have reality. What is there wrong or surprising, after all, in a boor behaving boorishly? See then if it is not rather yourself you ought to blame, for not foreseeing that he would offend in this way. You, in virtue of your reason, had every means for thinking it probable that he would do so; you forgot this, and now his offence takes you by surprise. When you are indignant with anyone for his perfidy or ingratitude, turn your thoughts first and foremost upon yourself. For the error is clearly your own, if you have put any faith in the good faith of a man of that stamp, or, when you have done him a kindness, if it was not done unreservedly and in the belief that the action would be its own full reward. Once you have done a man a service,

what more would you have? Is it not enough to have obeyed the laws of your own nature, without expecting to be paid for it? That is like the eye demanding a reward for seeing, or the feet for walking. It is for that very purpose that they exist; and they have their due in doing what they were created to do. Similarly, man is born for deeds of kindness; and when he has done a kindly action, or otherwise served the common welfare, he has done what he was made for, and has received his quittance.

Dio Cassius: The Advantage of Monarchy

One of the marked features of the second century A.D. was the spread of Roman citizenship and the increased participation of provincials in the processes of government. Among the beneficiaries of this development was Dio Cassius (ca. 160–230 A.D.), a Greek from Bithynia. The family from which he was sprung traveled in aristocratic circles in Bithynia and already possessed Roman citizenship. Dio himself went to Rome in 180 and pursued a full political career, sitting in the Roman senate, governing a province, and twice receiving appointment to the consulship. Like Polybius, another Greek who received intellectual stimulus at Rome, Dio combined the writing of history with the practical experience of the man of affairs. He undertook and completed an ambitious project: a history of Rome from its beginnings through his own day. The vast bulk of it is preserved, either in the original version or through lengthy excerpts by later Greek scholars. Naturally, the man whose family received the franchise through imperial policy and who was himself promoted to high office and prestige by the emperors found no fault with the system. In writing of Caesar's assassination, Dio uses the occasion to deliver an apologia for monarchy. The murder of Caesar, in the name of freedom, was a catastrophic error. Democracy has a pleasant ring, but can only bring discord and chaos. A vast empire, encompassing a conglomeration of peoples and ideas, needs firm guidance and control from the top. The system's merit can be measured by its success.

The following selection is from Dio, *Roman History*, Book XLIV, Secs. 1–2, trans. Earnest Cary in *Dio's Roman History, IV* (Cambridge, Mass.: Harvard University Press, 1961), 309–13. Reprinted by permission of the publishers and *The Loeb Classical Library*.

All this Caesar did as a preliminary step to his campaign against the Parthians; but a baleful frenzy which fell upon certain men through jealousy of his advancement and hatred of his preferment to themselves caused his death unlawfully, while it added a new name to the annals of infamy; it scattered the decrees to the winds and brought upon the Romans seditions and civil wars once more after a state of harmony. His slayers, to be sure, declared that they had shown themselves at once destroyers of Caesar and liberators of the people: but in reality they impiously plotted against him, and they threw the city into disorder when at last it possessed a stable government. Democracy, indeed, has a fair-appearing name and conveys the impression of bringing equal rights to all through equal laws, but its results are seen not to agree at all with its title. Monarchy, on the contrary, has an unpleasant sound, but is a most practical form of government to live under. For it is easier to find a single excellent man than many of them, and if even this seems to some a difficult feat, it is quite inevitable that the other alternative should be acknowledged to be impossible; for it does not belong to the majority of men to acquire virtue. And again, even though a base man should obtain supreme power, yet he is preferable to the masses of like character, as the history of the Greeks and barbarians and of the Romans themselves proves. For successes have always been greater and more frequent in the case both of cities and of individuals under kings than under popular rule, and disasters do [not] happen [so frequently] under monarchies as under mob-rule. Indeed, if ever there has been a prosperous democracy, it has in any case been at its best for only a brief period, so long, that is, as the people had neither the numbers nor the strength sufficient to cause insolence to spring up among them as the result of good fortune or jealousy as the result of ambition. But for a city, not only so large in itself, but also ruling the finest and the greatest part of the known world, holding sway over men of many and diverse natures, possessing many men of great wealth, occupied with every imaginable pursuit, enjoying every imaginable fortune, both individually and collectively,—for such a city, I say, to practise moderation under a democracy is impossible, and still more is it impossible for the people, unless moderation prevails, to be harmonious. Therefore, if Marcus Brutus and Gaius Cassius had only reflected upon these things, they would never have killed the city's head and protector nor have made themselves the cause of countless ills both to themselves and to all the rest of mankind then living.

Tacitus: *Dialogue on Orators*

Few will dispute the claim that Cornelius Tacitus (ca. 56–123 A.D.) was Rome's greatest historian. His searing portraits of the Julio-Claudians in *The Annales,* his last and most mature work, continue to dominate our conceptions of them. *The Annales,* together with the earlier *Histories,* formed a complete study of the period between the accession of Tiberius and the end of the Flavian dynasty. Tacitus had no peers in his compelling depictions of character and his searching analysis of the struggle between the early emperors and the Roman aristocracy. Writing, as he was, under Trajan and Hadrian, it was safe to express venom against the Julio-Claudians and Domitian. But the gloom and brooding pessimism that pervade Tacitus' work suggest that he was not altogether content with his contemporary circumstances. He knew too much about the past. Like his friend and correspondent Pliny, Tacitus pursued a distinguished public career in Rome, governed a province abroad, and reached the consulship at home. Also like Pliny he enjoyed a substantial reputation as an orator. Yet after ca. 100 A.D. Tacitus abandoned oratory for good. The *Dialogue on Orators* may contain a strong autobiographical element. It was constructed in the form of a simulated discussion, along the lines of Cicero's dialogues. The subject under scrutiny is the inferior quality of oratory under the empire when compared with the great days of the Republic. The final participant in the discussion, Maternus, obviously speaks with the voice of Tacitus. Republican oratory flourished in an era of turbulence and instability to which the great orators themselves contributed. The eloquence was powerful but disruptive, coincidental with civil strife. When monarchy came it brought peace and stability. There was no further need for persuasive speakers to stir the passions of the populace when the emperor made decisions and the law was supreme. Tacitus was no Republican. He recognized the benefits which the imperial rule had imposed. But there were sacrifices. The turbulence of the Republic was gone; but so was the stimulating atmosphere of the free state.

The following selection is from Tacitus, *Dialogue on Orators*, Secs. 36–41, trans. Moses Hadas in Moses Hadas, ed., *The Complete Works of Tacitus* (New York: The Modern Library, 1942), 764–69. Copyright 1942 by Random House, Inc. Reprinted by permission of Random House, Inc. and Alfred A. Knopf, Inc.

36. Great eloquence, like fire, grows with its material; it becomes fiercer with movement, and brighter as it burns. On this same principle was developed in our state too the eloquence of antiquity. Although even the modern orator has attained all that the circumstances of a settled, quiet, and prosperous community allow, still in the disorder and licence of the past more seemed to be within the reach of the speaker, when, amid a universal confusion that needed one guiding hand, he exactly adapted his wisdom to the bewildered people's capacity of conviction. Hence, laws without end and consequent popularity; hence, speeches of magistrates who, I may say, passed nights on the Rostra; hence, prosecutions of influential citizens brought to trial, and feuds transmitted to whole families; hence, factions among the nobles, and incessant strife between the senate and the people. In each case the state was torn asunder, but the eloquence of the age was exercised and, as it seemed, was loaded with great rewards. For the more powerful a man was as a speaker, the more easily did he obtain office, the more decisively superior was he to his colleagues in office, the more influence did he acquire with the leaders of the state, the more weight in the senate, the more notoriety and fame with the people. Such men had a host of clients, even among foreign nations; the magistrates, when leaving Rome for the provinces, showed them respect, and courted their favour as soon as they returned. The prætorship and the consulship seemed to offer them-

selves to them, and even when they were out of office, they were not out of power, for they swayed both people and senate with their counsels and influence. Indeed, they had quite convinced themselves that without eloquence no one could win or retain a distinguished and eminent position in the state. And no wonder. Even against their own wish they had to show themselves before the people. It was little good for them to give a brief vote in the senate without supporting their opinion with ability and eloquence. If brought into popular odium, or under some charge, they had to reply in their own words. Again, they were under the necessity of giving evidence in the public courts, not in their absence by affidavit, but of being present and of speaking it openly. There was thus a strong stimulus to win the great prizes of eloquence, and as the reputation of a good speaker was considered an honour and a glory, so it was thought a disgrace to seem mute and speechless. Shame therefore quite as much as hope of reward prompted men not to take the place of a pitiful client rather than that of a patron, or to see hereditary connections transferred to others, or to seem spiritless and incapable of office from either failing to obtain it or from holding it weakly when obtained.

37. Perhaps you have had in your hands the old records, still to be found in the libraries of antiquaries, which Mucianus is just now collecting, and which have already been brought together and published in, I think, eleven books of Transactions, and three of Letters. From these we may gather that Cneius Pompeius and Marcus Crassus rose to power as much by force of intellect and by speaking as by their might in arms; that the Lentuli, Metelli, Luculli, and Curios, and the rest of our nobles, bestowed great labour and pains on these studies, and that, in fact, no one in those days acquired much influence without some eloquence. We must consider too the eminence of the men accused, and the vast issues involved. These of themselves do very much for eloquence. There is, indeed, a wide difference between having to speak on a theft, a technical point, a judicial decision, and on bribery at elections, the plundering of the allies, and the massacre of citizens. Though it is better that these evils should not befall us, and the best condition of the state is that in which we are spared such sufferings, still, when they did occur, they supplied a grand material for the orator. His mental powers rise with the dignity of his subject, and no one can produce a noble and brilliant speech unless he has

got an adequate case. Demosthenes, I take it, does not owe his fame to his speeches against his guardians, and it is not his defence of Publius Quintius, or of Licinius Archias, which make Cicero a great orator; it is his Catiline, his Milo, his Verres, and Antonius, which have shed over him this lustre. Not indeed that it was worth the state's while to endure bad citizens that orators might have plenty of matter for their speeches, but, as I now and then remind you, we must remember the point, and understand that we are speaking of an art which arose more easily in stormy and unquiet times. Who knows not that it is better and more profitable to enjoy peace than to be harassed by war? Yet war produces more good soldiers than peace. Eloquence is on the same footing. The oftener she has stood, so to say, in the battle-field, the more wounds she has inflicted and received, the mightier her antagonist, the sharper the conflicts she has freely chosen, the higher and more splendid has been her rise, and ennobled by these contests she lives in the praises of mankind.

38. I pass now to the forms and character of procedure in the old courts. As they exist now, they are indeed more favourable to truth, but the forum in those days was a better training for eloquence. There no speaker was under the necessity of concluding within a very few hours; there was freedom of adjournment, and every one fixed for himself the limits of his speech, and there was no prescribed number of days or of counsel. It was Cneius Pompeius who, in his third consulship, first restricted all this, and put a bridle, so to say, on eloquence, intending, however, that all business should be transacted in the forum according to law, and before the prætors. Here is a stronger proof of the greater importance of the cases tried before these judges than in the fact that causes in the Court of the Hundred, causes which now hold the first place, were then so eclipsed by the fame of other trials that not a speech of Cicero, or Cæsar, or Brutus, or Caelius, or Calvus, or, in short, any great orator is now read, that was delivered in that Court, except only the orations of Asinius Pollio for the heirs of Urbinia, as they are entitled, and even Pollio delivered these in the middle of the reign of Augustus, a period of long rest, of unbroken repose for the people and tranquillity for the senate, when the emperor's perfect discipline had put its restraints on eloquence as well as on all else.

39. Perhaps what I am going to say will be thought trifling and

ridiculous; but I will say it even to be laughed at. What contempt (so I think at least) has been brought on eloquence by those little overcoats into which we squeeze, and, so to say, box ourselves up, when we chat with the judges! How much force may we suppose has been taken from our speeches by the little rooms and offices in which nearly all cases have to be set forth. Just as a spacious course tests a fine horse, so the orator has his field, and unless he can move in it freely and at ease, his eloquence grows feeble and breaks down. Nay more; we find the pains and labour of careful composition out of place, for the judge keeps asking when you are going to open the case, and you must begin from his question. Frequently he imposes silence on the advocate to hear proofs and witnesses. Meanwhile only one or two persons stand by you as you are speaking and the whole business is transacted almost in solitude. But the orator wants shouts and applause, and something like a theatre, all which and the like were the every day lot of the orators of antiquity, when both numbers and nobility pressed into the forum, when gatherings of clients and the people in their tribes and deputations from the towns and indeed a great part of Italy stood by the accused in his peril, and Rome's citizens felt in a multitude of trials that they themselves had an interest in the decision. We know that there was a universal rush of the people to hear the accusation and the defence of Cornelius, Scaurus, Milo, Bestia, and Vatinius, so that even the coldest speaker might have been stirred and kindled by the mere enthusiasm of the citizens in their strife. And therefore indeed such pleadings are still extant, and thus the men too who pleaded, owe their fame to no other speeches more than these.

40. Again, what stimulus to genius and what fire to the orator was furnished by incessant popular assemblies, by the privilege of attacking the most influential men, and by the very glory of such feuds when most of the good speakers did not spare even a Publius Scipio, or a Sulla, or a Cneius Pompeius, and following the common impulse of envy availed themselves of the popular ear for invective against eminent citizens. I am not speaking of a quiet and peaceful accomplishment, which delights in what is virtuous and well regulated. No; the great and famous eloquence of old is the nursling of the license which fools called freedom; it is the companion of sedition, the stimulant of an unruly people, a stranger to obedience and subjection, a defiant, reckless, presumptuous

thing which does not show itself in a well-governed state. What orator have we ever heard of at Sparta or at Crete? A very strict discipline and very strict laws prevailed, tradition says, in both those states. Nor do we know of the existence of eloquence among the Macedonians or Persians, or in any people content with a settled government. There were some orators at Rhodes and a host of them at Athens, but there the people, there any ignorant fellow, anybody, in short, could do anything. So too our own state, while it went astray and wore out its strength in factious strife and discord, with neither peace in the forum, unity in the senate, order in the courts, respect for merit, or seemly behaviour in the magistrates, produced beyond all question a more vigorous eloquence, just as an untilled field yields certain herbage in special plenty. Still the eloquence of the Gracchi was not an equivalent to Rome for having to endure their legislation, and Cicero's fame as an orator was a poor compensation for the death he died.

41. And so now the forum, which is all that our speakers have left them of antiquity, is an evidence of a state not thoroughly reformed or as orderly as we could wish. Who but the guilty or unfortunate apply to us? What town puts itself under our protection but one harassed by its neighbours or by strife at home? When we plead for a province, is it not one that has been plundered and ill-treated? Surely it would be better not to complain than to have to seek redress. Could a community be found in which no one did wrong, an orator would be as superfluous among its innocent people as a physician among the healthy. As the healing art is of very little use and makes very little progress in nations which enjoy particularly robust constitutions and vigorous frames, so the orator gets an inferior and less splendid renown where a sound morality and willing obedience to authority prevail. What need there of long speeches in the senate, when the best men are soon of one mind, or of endless harangues to the people, when political questions are decided not by an ignorant multitude, but by one man of pre-eminent wisdom? What need of voluntary prosecutions, when crimes are so rare and slight, or of defences full of spiteful insinuation and exceeding proper bounds, when the clemency of the judge offers itself to the accused in his peril?

Be assured, my most excellent, and, as far as the age requires, most eloquent friends, that had you been born in the past, and the men we admire in our own day, had some god in fact sud-

denly changed your lives and your age, the highest fame and glory
of eloquence would have been yours, and they too would not have
lacked moderation and self-control. As it is, seeing that no one can
at the same time enjoy great renown and great tranquillity, let
everybody make the best of the blessings of his own age without
disparaging other periods.

Maternus had now finished. There were, replied Messala, some
points I should controvert, some on which I should like to hear
more, if the day were not almost spent. It shall be, said Maternus,
as you wish, on a future occasion, and anything you have thought
obscure in my argument, we will again discuss. Then he rose and
embraced Aper. I mean, he said, to accuse you before the poets,
and so will Messala before the antiquarians. And I, rejoined Aper,
will accuse you before the rhetoricians and professors.

They laughed good-humouredly, and we parted.

Juvenal: *Fourth Satire*

The somber pessimism detectable in Tacitus is even more
prominent in the poems of his contemporary Decimus
Junius Juvenalis (ca. 60–131 A.D.). Rome never produced a
more penetrating writer of satiric poetry. The satirist's eye
is quick to catch the foibles of his age. Juvenal trained his
fire on all imaginable types: the politician, the tradesman,
the nouveau riche, the writer, the philosopher, the informer,
the sycophant, the freedman, the immigrant, the emanci-
pated woman. The picture is dark and devastating. Nor did
the emperor himself escape. Like Tacitus and Pliny, Juvenal
came to maturity under Domitian, but did not venture to
publish until the reign of Trajan, when it was safe and expected to denounce the former emperor. Juvenal's verses
contain bitter and biting invectives against Domitian and
his toadies. Most revealing is the brilliant satire on the
emperor's privy council or *consilium*. That institution was
no novelty. The employment of friends and trusted ad-
visors as an informal policy group was an old practice,
dating back to Augustus, and continued to be used by the

Antonines. Juvenal depicts Domitian's *consilium* as debating the fate of an oversized fish. The issue is treated as the most solemn matter of state: the ministers themselves are cringing stooges, pale, nervous, and terrified; the tyrant, unconcerned with the great matters of empire, languishes in luxury and gluttony, dependent upon the vilest creatures to make his decisions, and fritters away imperial resources on trivia. That this was just personal vendetta against Domitian is unlikely. Juvenal knew that some of Domitian's counselors retained their positions under Trajan. The satirist's malaise was deep.

The following selection is from Juvenal, *Satire IV*, trans. Hubert Creekmore in *The Satires of Juvenal* (New York: Mentor Books, 1963), pp. 63–71. Reprinted by permission of The New American Library, Inc.

Look here, once again Crispinus!
    I'll often have to call
Him onto my stage, this monster of
    evil without one small
Redeeming virtue, this low debauchee,
    diseased and dread,
Strong only in lust that scorns no
    one except the unwed.
What does it matter, then, how big
    are the colonnades
That tire his horses, how broad the
    woods where he drives in shade,
How many lots near the forum, how many
    mansions, he's bought?
No bad man is happy, least of all a
    seducer who's brought
To incest, with whom a filleted
    priestess lately has lain,
To be, for that, interred while blood
    still pulsed in her veins.

But to lighter matters. Although if
    another had done the same,
He'd fall in the censor's grasp; for
    what would be called a shame
In Tom, Dick, or Harry became in
    Crispinus simply a grace.

What can you do when any charge you
    can bring him to face
Is less dreadful and foul than the
    man himself? He bought a mullet
For three hundred dollars—something
    like fifty a pound, as they would put it
Who want to exaggerate and make up
    a real fish tale.
I'd praise the cunning of his schemes
    if he prevailed
By any such costly gift upon a
    childless old man
To name him first in his will, or
    for better reasons, planned
To send it to some fine doxy who
    shuns the public glance
Behind shades of a litter with
    picture windows. Not a chance:
He bought it all for himself. We see
    a lot of things done
Today that the frugal glutton Apicius
    would have shunned.
Crispinus, did you, who formerly
    wore a G-string supplied
By your native papyrus, pay that price
    for a fish? You might
Have purchased the fisherman himself
    perhaps for less
Than the fish; and for the same amount
    you could possess
A farm in the provinces or a bigger
    estate like those
Down in Apulia. What sort of feasts
    must we suppose
The emperor himself gobbled up
    when by a parasite duke
In purple of palace pomp those hundreds
    of bucks were puked—
A mere appetizer, that fish, hors-d'oeuvre
    in a modest feast.
This man's now chief of the knights,
    who once was only too pleased
To sell his Egyptian brothers, yelling,
    "Mudcats for sale!"

Begin, Calliope! Here's no lyric for
    song; a tale
That's true is to be the subject.
    Now let's take our seats.
Pierian maidens, recount the story.
    And in that I treat
You to the name of maiden, may I be
    profited.

When the last of the Flavians was flaying
    a world half dead,
And Rome was slave to a baldheaded
    Nero, there appeared
In a net in the Adriatic, before the
    shrine that's reared
To Venus high over Greek Ancona, a
    turbot whose size
Was gigantic. It bulged at the
    meshes—a fish as much a prize
As those the Sea of Azov hides under
    ice till the sun
Cracks open the crust, and sluggish
    but fat from cold, they run
To the rushing Black Sea's mouth.
    The skipper means this whale
Of a fish for the chief pontiff—for
    who'd dare put on sale
Or buy so big a fish when even the
    beaches were thick
With informers? Customs men, inspecting
    seaweed, would be quick
To dash off and charge the helpless
    fisher, with no qualms
At swearing the fish long fattened in
    Caesar's ponds, therefrom
Escaped, and must be returned to its
    former lord. If we come
To believe what's held by Armillatus
    or Palfurius,
Everything that swims, is delicious,
    rare, or curious,
In any ocean whatever, belongs to the
    royal purse.
So, lest it go to waste, it shall be
    a gift he confers.

By now unwholesome autumn was yielding
    to frost at last,
Malarial patients hoped for relief,
    and cold winter's blast
Kept the fish quite fresh. And yet
    he hurried as if the hot
South Wind were dogging his heels.
    And when he'd gone somewhat
Past the lake where Alba, though ruined,
    tends the Trojan flame
And prays in the smaller temple of
    Vesta, a crowd that came
In wonder blocked his passage a while;
    and as it withdrew,
The gates on easy hinges swung out;
    and the senators who
Were excluded stared at the fish that
    got in. And it was sped
To this son of Atreus. Then the man
    of Picenum said:
"Accept a fish far too big for a
    mortal's kitchen. Declare
This a festival day. Make haste to
    vomit all that rich fare
In your stomach and eat a turbot
    preserved for your own reign.
The fish itself desired to be caught."
    What could be more inane,
More barefaced? And yet King Rooster's
    comb began to rise
With delight; when his power's
    praised as equal to that in the skies,
There's nothing a godlike emperor can't
    believe of himself.
But no dish big enough for the fish
    could be found on any shelf!

So the chief advisers were called
    into council—men he hated,
Upon whose faces was spread the ashen
    fear created
By his great and dangerous friendship.
    The first to rush
At the steward's call, "Hurry up, he's
    waiting!" was Pegasus,

Pulling on a snatched-up robe; for
    recently he'd been
Appointed as bailiff over the stunned
    city. Back then,
What else would a prefect be? But
    he was the best of the lot,
The most just interpreter of the law,
    although he thought,
In even those vicious times, that
    justice should not be dealt
By swords. Then came delightful old
    Crispus, whose unexcelled
And gentle spirit was equalled by
    his eloquent speech.
What better adviser for the monarch
    of the whole reach
Of oceans, lands, and nations if
    only he had been free,
Under that scourge and plague, to
    condemn his brutality
And give good moral advice? But what's
    more dangerous to men
Than the ear of a tyrant, upon whose
    whim the fate of a friend
Who spoke of showers, the heat, the
    rainy spring, depends?
So he never swam against the tide,
    nor was he such
A citizen as could utter the freeborn
    thoughts that touched
His heart, or risk his life for truth.
    He lived in this way
Through many winters and on to his
    eightieth birthday,
Protected in even that court by weapons
    like these from harm.

Behind him hurried Acilius, a man the
    same age, at his arm
The son who did not deserve the cruel
    death in store,
So quickly rushed upon him by his
    ruler's swords.
But to be both old and noble has become
    long since

The same as being a prodigy; it follows,
    hence,
That I'd rather be a clod, baby
    brother of giants, than those.
It was no help, therefore, to his
    wretched son that in close
Combat, as a naked huntsman, he speared
    Numidian bears
In the Alban arena. For who would
    not nowadays be aware
Of patrician tricks? Who'd think that
    old-fashioned ruse you achieved,
Brutus, was wonderful? Kings wearing
    beards are easily deceived.

With no happier face, though of ignoble
    bloodlines, Rubrius came—
Condemned long ago of crime no one
    mentions, yet deeper in shame
Than a satire-writing pervert. Then
    appeared the gluttonous belly
Of Montanus, and slightly later
    Montanus himself; and smelly
Crispinus, exuding at early daybreak
    enough strong scent
To outsmell two funerals. More
    vicious than he, next went
Pompeius, who had a tender whisper
    that slit men's throats;
And Fuscus, who, planning wars in his
    marble halls, would devote
His guts to Romanian vultures.
    Cautious Veiento in turn
Arrived with lethal Catullus, who with
    passion burned
For a girl he'd never seen—in even
    our time a great
And notable marvel, a blind sycophant,
    a dread courtier straight
From the beggars' bridges, worthy to
    beg at chariot wheels
And blow soft kisses to those descending
    the Arician hill.
No one was more amazed at the fish,
    for he said a great deal

About it, turning left. But the
    creature lay to his right.
In the same way, he'd praise a Cilician
    gladiator's fight
Or the hoist that snatches boy actors
    up into the flies.

But Veiento will not be outdone. Like
    a seer who prophesies
When nipped, O Bellona, by your gadfly,
    in frenzy he cries:
"An omen divine you have here, of a
    brilliant, great victory!
You'll capture some barbarous king,
    or Prince Arviragus will be
Knocked out of his British car and die.
    This beast, I opine,
Is of foreign birth. For see you not
    along the spine
Those spearlike fins?" There was nothing
    left for Fabricius, then,
Except to mention the turbot's age
    and its origin.

"Then what's your advice?" the emperor
    asked. "Cut it in two?"
"Heaven forfend," said Montanus; "such
    indignity will not do!
Command a deep vessel to be molded,
    of size so immense
Its thin walls can fitly embrace his
    gigantic circumference.
For the dish a great and instant
    Prometheus must come!
Make haste with clay, with wheel!
    But henceforth, O Caesar, let some
Good potters always attend your camp."
    This proposal, suited
Well to the man, won out. The old
    dissipations rooted
Deep in the royal court he knew, and
    Nero's soirées
That lasted beyond midnight, till a
    second hunger was raised
Inside them, when the blood by Falernian
    wine was heated.

No one in my time had greater knowledge
    of eating than he did.
He knew at the first bite if an oyster
    was born on a bed
In the Lucrine Bay, on Campania's
    rocks, or had been sped
From Kent; a glance revealed the coast
    where a sea urchin was bred.

The session's adjourned and the
    councillors are sent outside
Whom the mighty monarch had dragged
    posthaste and terrified
To his Alban palace as though he'd
    give them news of fierce
Germanic tribes on the warpath, or
    there had come to his ears,
With the speed of carrier pigeons flown
    from the faraway
Outposts of the empire, some quite
    alarming communiqué.

Even so, if only he had devoted to
    trifling nonsense
Like this all those days of cruelty
    and violence
When he robbed the city of its most
    noble and brilliant souls,
Unpunished, with none to avenge!
    But once he began to hold
Great terror for men in the lower
    classes, he was killed,
Soaked in the noble Lamian blood
    that he had spilled.

Part Five

THE EMPIRE AND
ITS SUBJECTS

Hitherto the image of Rome has been seen through the eyes of Romans or those whose source of inspiration was Rome. But the city-state had long ago outgrown its origins. Rome was the center and controlling agent of a vast network which comprised Spaniards, Gauls, Greeks, North Africans, and Orientals. The imperial establishment governed a mixed bag of peoples, cities, leagues, and empires. What was the reaction of the provincial populace to the rule of Rome? As one can imagine, the responses were also mixed. We are not blessed with an abundance of material stemming from Rome's foreign dependencies, but a few examples can provide much illumination.

Vergil had sung that Rome humbled the mighty but spared the weak. In the era of the Caesars, Rome gradually ceased to be a conqueror and became an administrator. She could claim, justifiably, the settling of foreign conflicts and the expansion of a uniform and stable system. The provinces received a more regular and systematic organization. Governors were appointed by the emperor and remained at their task for longer periods of time. Salaried officials, responsible to the throne, began to appear in larger numbers. A bureaucracy gave to the system a more permanent structure. Most important, the distinction between Roman and provincial progressively disappeared. The extension of Roman citizenship was the principal vehicle. It not only spread the franchise and civil rights, but soon brought former provincials into the governing process as officials, administrators, and even senators. For many these developments were salutary and called forth praise and gratitude. For others, however, they did not outweigh the presence of Roman authority and the subjection of their native states.

The extension of citizenship to the Gauls, once Rome's most redoubtable foes, bore fruit already in the early empire. By the reign of Claudius, Gallic aristocrats, who had enjoyed the franchise for more than a generation, were prepared to enter the Roman senate. Claudius himself supported their cause: the senate could now more closely approximate a body representative of the empire. Provincial aristocrats elsewhere also welcomed the power and suzerainty of Rome. Even in Judaea, where Rome met the most recalcitrant opposition, the Jewish general and historian Josephus berated his countrymen for their obstinate resistance and their failure to recognize the benefits of Roman rule. From the Greek world came the rhetorician Aelius Aristides, who delivered praise in effusive language. His eulogy of Rome portrays a unified empire stretching through most of the known world, bound together by common citizenship and peaceful commerce, protected by valiant legions, and under the benevolent leadership of worthy rulers.

The panegyrics leave out of account subject peoples who chafed under Roman rule and the works of whose spokesmen were not permitted wide circulation. The *Acts of the Pagan Martyrs* reveal a bitter anti-Semitic and anti-Roman tradition based in Alexandria. And not all Jewish intellectuals pursued the line of Josephus. Much of the corpus of Sibylline Oracles which has come down to us was compiled by Jews who put their apocalyptic visions in pagan dress and predicted the violent destruction of the Roman empire. Selections from Tacitus' *Histories* conclude the section. Through speeches put in the mouths of German and Roman leaders respectively Tacitus sums up the arguments on both sides regarding the effects of Roman rule. Provincials might see it as the imposition of slavery; Romans preferred to stress the blessings of unity.

Claudius: *Speech on Gallic Senators*

The Emperor Claudius was born at Lyons in Gaul. That was accident, not nationality. His father was serving in the area at that time. But a fondness for Gaul remained. In 48 A.D. the emperor advocated the inclusion of Gauls into the Roman senate. Resistance emerged, but the move was part of a logical development. Claudius was not supporting the claims of Gallic revolutionaries, but of aristocrats and leaders who could count a tradition of Roman citizenship in their families. Opposition spokesmen in the senate raised fears which smacked of racism and pointed to the history of Rome's wars with Gaul. Claudius' speech in reply proved more persuasive: the Gallic wars were ancient history; Gaul had flourished in peace and benefited the empire; her leaders were loyal Romans. And there was a larger justification: Rome had grown great through allowing an ever-wider participation in the governmental process. New blood should be judged on its talent and its loyalty, not on its origins. Claudius' speech was inscribed in bronze and a copy was recovered and preserved from Lyons. The remaining portions are not complete, but Tacitus also has a version in the *Annals,* based on the inscription but paraphrased in inimitable Tacitean style. The emperor, of course, had his way. The admission of a bloc of Gallic nobles to the senate stimulated and hastened a process which was to reach full fruition in the Antonine age: the regular involvement of gifted or favored men of provincial origins in the decisions of government.

The following translation of Claudius' speech to the Gauls is by E. G. Hardy in *Three Spanish Charters and Other Documents* (London: Oxford University Press, 1912), 147 54. Reprinted by permission of the Clarendon Press. The second selection is from Tacitus, *Annals,* Book XI, Secs. 23–25, trans. Moses Hadas in Moses Hadas, ed., *The Complete Works of Tacitus* (New York: The Modern Library, 1942), 240–42. Copyright 1942 by Random House, Inc. Reprinted by permission of Random House, Inc. and Alfred A. Knopf, Inc.

. . . may be useful to the commonwealth. And indeed, looking to the very first and foremost impression in the minds of the public, which I foresee will meet me at the very outset, I beg of you not to be startled at my proposal, as at the introduction of a new precedent, but much rather to reflect how many new precedents have taken their place in our constitution, and into how many forms and phases from the first origin of our city our republic has been made to fit.

There was a time when kings possessed this city, without however being able to hand it down to successors within their own families. Others took their place from other families and even from other nations. Thus Numa succeeded Romulus, imported from the Sabines, a neighbor it is true, but of a foreign stock. Thus Priscus Tarquinius succeeded Ancus Martius. The former, born at Tarquinii, of Demaratus, a Corinthian, and a high-born mother of that city, . . . poor she must have been, to be compelled to marry such a husband . . . he, I say, being precluded through the taint in his blood from obtaining honors in his own home, migrated to Rome, and obtained the position of king. Between him again and his son or grandson, for on this point our authorities disagree, there intervened Servius Tullius, sprung, if we believe our own historians, from a captive woman named Ocresia. According to Tuscan writers, I may remind you, he was once the loyal and devoted retainer of Caelius Vivenna, whose every fortune he shared, and when by changing fortune he was driven to leave Etruria with all that was left of the army of Caelius, he occupied the Caelian Mount, giving it this name from his leader Caelius, and changing his own name from the Tuscan form, Mastarna, assumed that by which we know him. At any rate, as I have said, he obtained the position of king, with the greatest advantage to the State. Later on, when the habits of Tarquinius Superbus, and no less of his sons, became hateful to our State, the minds of the people grew weary of the kingship, and the administration of the republic was transferred to the annual magistrates whom we call consuls.

What need now for me to remind you how the dictatorship was contrived by our ancestors, a power greater even than that of the consuls, to be made use of in more dangerous wars or more threatening civil commotion? Or how the tribunes were created to give protection to the plebs? What need to cite the transfer of power from consuls to decemviri, and its restoration once more to the consuls, when that tenfold kingship was broken up? Why should I recall how the consular power was divided among a larger number, the so-called military tribunes with consular power, who were elected, six or sometimes eight, each year? And how at last the privilege was shared with the plebs of holding not only magistracies, but also priesthoods? Indeed, if I should tell the story of our wars from their beginnings under our ancestors to the point we have reached to-day, I fear lest I should be thought arrogant, nay, should seem to have sought occasion to boast the glory of our empire's extension beyond the limits of the ocean. I will rather return to the point. Our citizenship. . . .

*   *   *

. . . can be done. It was, we know, an innovation when my great-uncle, the divine Augustus, and my uncle, Tiberius Caesar, decided that the better and wealthier members, the flower of the colonies and municipia throughout the empire, should have a place within this Senate House. But you ask me; has not an Italian a better claim than a provincial? That question I shall answer by the selection I make, when I come to justify to you that part of my censorship. Meanwhile, in my opinion, not even provincial senators are to be excluded, provided that they are qualified to adorn this House.

Look, I pray you, at that most splendid and powerful colony of Vienne, and remember for how long a time it has furnished senators to this House. From that colony came L. Vestinus, one of the chief ornaments of the equestrian order, whom I value among my most intimate friends, and whose services I still monopolize, for my own affairs. But it is my desire to see his children obtain the highest among priestly offices and proceed, as their years advance, to the further stages of their career. An ill-omened name occurs to me—a ruffian bore it—, and I pass it over. Besides, I hate that blend of the gymnast and the "rara avis," who imported the consulship into his family, even before his colony had received the full privilege of the Roman citizenship. I might say the same of the man's brother, though he is prevented by a pitiable and undeserved fate from proving himself a useful senator. But now that you have come, Ti. Caesar Germanicus, to the extreme boundaries of Gallia Narbonensis, it is full time that you should disclose to the conscript fathers the purpose of your address.

I say this: these illustrious youths whom I see before me, will no more give you cause for regret, if I make them senators, than my noble friend Persicus has cause for regret, when he recognizes among the ancestral images of his family the name of Allobrogicus. But if you admit that these things are so, what more do you demand than that I should point to this one fact, that the regions beyond Gallia Narbonensis already send us senators, since we have and do not regret to have men among our order from Lugudunum. It is with some hesitation, conscript fathers, that I have passed outside the limits of your well-known and familiar provinces, but the time has come when I must plead in no uncertain tones the cause of Gallia Comata. And if any among you looks to this, that these people defied the divine Julius in war for ten whole years, let him put against that the unswerving loyalty and obedience of a hundred years, tested and tested again by many a critical moment in our fortunes. It was they who, during his task of subduing Germany, afforded my father Drusus by their tranquillity a steady peace and security in his rear, and that at a time when he had been called away to the war from the work, still strange and new to the Gauls, of imposing the census. How arduous that work still is today at the present moment, among ourselves, although nothing is required from us beyond a public knowledge of our material resources, I have the best reason to know from only too clear proofs.

Tacitus: *Annals*

23. In the consulship of Aulus Vitellius and Lucius Vipstanus the question of filling up the Senate was discussed, and the chief men of Gallia Comata, as it was called, who had long possessed the rights of allies and of Roman citizens, sought the privilege of obtaining public offices at Rome. There was much talk of every

kind on the subject, and it was argued before the emperor with vehement opposition. "Italy," it was asserted,

is not so feeble as to be unable to furnish its own capital with a senate. Once our native-born citizens sufficed for peoples of our own kin, and we are by no means dissatisfied with the Rome of the past. To this day we cite examples, which under our old customs the Roman character exhibited as to valour and renown. Is it a small thing that Veneti and Insubres have already burst into the Senate-house, unless a mob of foreigners, a troop of captives, so to say, is now forced upon us? What distinctions will be left for the remnants of our noble houses, or for any impoverished senators from Latium? Every place will be crowded with these millionaires, whose ancestors of the second and third generations at the head of hostile tribes destroyed our armies with fire and sword, and actually besieged the divine Julius at Alesia. These are recent memories. What if there were to rise up the remembrance of those who fell in Rome's citadel and at her altar by the hands of these same barbarians! Let them enjoy indeed the title of citizens, but let them not vulgarise the distinctions of the Senate and the honours of office.

24. These and like arguments failed to impress the emperor. He at once addressed himself to answer them, and thus harangued the assembled Senate.

My ancestors, the most ancient of whom was made at once a citizen and a noble of Rome, encourage me to govern by the same policy of transferring to this city all conspicuous merit, wherever found. And indeed I know, as facts, that the Julii came from Alba, the Coruncanii from Camerium, the Porcii from Tusculum, and not to inquire too minutely into the past, that new members have been brought into the Senate from Etruria and Lucania and the whole of Italy, that Italy itself was at last extended to the Alps, to the end that not only single persons but entire countries and tribes might be united under our name. We had unshaken peace at home; we prospered in all our foreign relations, in the days when Italy beyond the Po was admitted to share our citizenship, and when, enrolling in our ranks the most vigorous of the provincials, under colour of settling our legions throughout the world, we recruited our exhausted empire. Are we sorry that the Balbi came to us from Spain, and other men not less illustrious from Narbon Gaul? Their descendants are still among us, and do not yield to us in patriotism. What was the ruin of Sparta and Athens, but this, that mighty as they were in war, they spurned from them as aliens those whom they had conquered? Our founder Romulus, on the other hand, was so wise that he fought as enemies and then hailed as fellow-citizens several nations on the very same day. Strangers have reigned over us. That freedmen's sons should be intrusted with public offices is not, as many wrongly think, a sudden innovation, but was a common practice in the old commonwealth. But, it will be said, we have fought with the Senones. I suppose then that the Volsci and Æqui never stood in array against us. Our city was taken by the Gauls. Well, we also gave hostages to the Etruscans, and passed under the yoke of the Samnites. On the whole, if you review all our wars, never has one been finished in a shorter time than that with the Gauls. Thenceforth they have preserved an unbroken and loyal peace. United as they now are with us by manners, education, and intermarriage, let them bring us their gold and their wealth rather than enjoy it in isolation. Everything, Senators, which we now hold to be of the highest antiquity, was once new. Plebeian magistrates came after patrician; Latin magistrates after plebeian; magistrates of other Italian peoples after Latin. This practice too will establish itself, and what we are this day justifying by precedents, will be itself a precedent.

25. The emperor's speech was followed by a decree of the Senate, and the Ædui were the first to obtain the right of becoming senators at Rome. This compliment was paid to their ancient alliance, and to the fact that they alone of the Gauls cling to the name of brothers of the Roman people.

About the same time the emperor enrolled in the ranks of the patricians such senators as were of the oldest families, and such as had had distinguished ancestors. There were now but scanty relics of the Greater Houses of Romulus and of the Lesser Houses of Lucius Brutus, as they had been called, and those too were exhausted which the Dictator Cæsar by the Cassian and the emperor Augustus by the Sænian law had chosen into their place. These acts, as being welcome to the State, were undertaken with hearty gladness by the imperial censor. Anxiously considering how he was to rid the Senate of men of notorious infamy, he preferred a gentle method, recently devised, to one which accorded with the sternness of antiquity, and advised each to examine his own case and seek the privilege of laying aside his rank. Permission, he said, would be readily obtained. He would publish in the same list those who had been expelled and those who had been allowed to retire, that by this confounding together of the decision of the censors and the modesty of voluntary resignation the disgrace might be softened.

For this, the consul Vipstanus moved that Claudius should be called "Father of the Senate." The title of "Father of the Country" had, he argued, been indiscriminately bestowed; new services ought to be recognised by unusual titles. The emperor however himself stopped the consul's flattery, as extravagant.

Josephus: The Jewish War

Roman relations with the Jews periodically fluctuated between cordiality and explosion. The Jews generally enjoyed religious freedom in the empire, but rapacious governors or megalomaniacal rulers could drive Judaea to the brink of revolution. Insofar as Roman policy was successful, it was due to Hellenized Jewish leaders who preferred a cosmopolitan to an exclusively nationalistic outlook and who advocated peaceful collaboration with Rome. One such was Herod Agrippa, a Jewish prince who was also friend and companion of Roman emperors. Another was Josephus (ca. 37–115 A.D.), who descended from a noble priestly family and had a strong training in both Jewish antiquities and Greek learning. When Judaea erupted in revolt against Rome in 66, Josephus, as befitted his rank, served in a command position in Galilee. But his heart was not in rebellion. The war had broken that harmonious cooperation between Rome and Judaea which Josephus regarded as the proper order of the universe. He was himself captured by the Roman general Vespasian and brought to Rome. When Vespasian ascended the throne and sent his son Titus to continue the war, Josephus was in Titus' entourage with the task of persuading his countrymen to yield. After the war he pursued his work in Rome, under the generous patronage of the emperors, and took up the task of justifying the ways of Rome to Judaea. The result

was his *Bellum Judaicum* (*The Jewish War*). The following
passage gives his own speech to the defenders of Jerusalem,
urging them to eschew fruitless resistance and to acknowledge
the advantages of Roman suzerainty. The history of Roman
success, so the historian stresses, demonstrates that God
himself has enlisted on the side of Rome and the future.

The following selection is from Josephus, *The Jewish War*,
Book V, Ch. 9, Secs. 3–4, trans. Nahum N. Glatzer in *Jerusalem
and Rome, The Writings of Josephus* (Cleveland: World Publishing Company, 1960), 248–56. Reprinted by permission of
World Publishing Company and William Collins Sons & Co., Ltd.

So Josephus circled the wall, endeavoring to find a spot
out of range of the missiles that would at the same time, be within
hearing distance; and at great length entreated them to spare themselves, the people, their country, and their temple, and not to mani-
fest greater indifference in these matters than did aliens.

The Romans, he said, though they had no part in them, respected the sacred rites and places of their foes and had thus far
withheld their hands from them; while those who had been reared
among them, who alone would enjoy them were they preserved,
were bent on their destruction. Indeed, their firmest walls they
saw prostrate, and that alone remaining which was weaker than
what has been taken. They knew that the power of the Romans
was invincible and that to serve them was no new experience. If,
indeed, to wage war for freedom is noble, that should have been
done earlier; but having once succumbed, and for so long a period
submitted, then to cast off the yoke was the deed not of lovers of
liberty but of men madly courting death.

To disdain ignoble masters was perhaps admissible; but not
those who ruled the world. For what had escaped the Romans,
except perhaps some spot made valueless through heat or cold?
Fortune had on all sides been transferred to the Romans, and God,
who had bestowed power on all the nations in turn, now rested
over Italy. It was an established law, and of the greatest force
among brute beasts as well as men, to yield to the stronger, and
that dominion should belong to those who are supreme in arms.

Accordingly, their ancestors, who were much superior in mind
and body, as well as in resources generally, had yet submitted to

the Romans, which they would not have done had they not known that God was with the Romans. As for themselves what did they rely on in holding out, when most of their city was already taken, and when they, though their walls were still intact, were enduring calamities worse than capture? For it did not escape the Romans that famine raged in the city, a famine that was now consuming the people and would soon consume the men in arms as well. For even should the Romans raise the siege and not attack the city sword in hand, a war beyond the strife of arms was besetting them from within and would with each hour gather strength unless the ability were theirs to wield weapons and wage war against famine, or unless they alone among mankind could subdue even the claims of nature.

He added further that it would be well to alter their conduct before their miseries became incurable and to resort to salutary counsels while the opportunity still remained. The Romans would bear no grudge against them for their past deeds if they persisted not in their contumacy, for the Romans were by nature lenient in victory and preferred what was expedient to the gratification of their passions. And how would it advantage them to possess a city devoid of inhabitants and a desert region? For these reasons, Titus, even at this late date, wished to offer them terms. But if he took the city by storm, he would slaughter them to a man, especially if they rejected his offers in this, their direst, distress. That the third wall would be speedily taken, those already fallen gave proof. And even were that bulwark impregnable, the famine would fight for the Romans against them.

As he thus exhorted them, Josephus was by many derided from the wall, railed at by many others, and assailed with missiles by some. On finding his direct advice disregarded, he passed to the history of their nation.

"Miserable men!" he cried.

Are you so unmindful of your own true allies as to wage war against the Romans with weapons and your hands? What other nation have we vanquished by such means? When did God, who created, fail to avenge the Jews if they were wronged? Will you not look back and consider what that place is whence you issue to battle and how mighty an Ally you have outraged? Will you not recall the superhuman exploits of your forefathers and what mighty foes this holy place has in bygone days destroyed for us?

As for me, I shudder when declaring the works of God to such unworthy ears. Listen, nevertheless, that you may know that you war not only against the Romans but against God himself. Necoh, king of Egypt, who bore also the name Pharaoh, came with a prodigious army and carried off queen Sarah, the mother of our nation. What did her husband, Abraham, our forefather, do then? Though he had three hundred and eighteen officers, each commanding a countless host, did he take vengeance on this tyrant with the sword? Or did he not rather deem these soldiers as nothing if unaided by God, and lifting pure hands towards this holy site, which you have now polluted, enlist the invincible Supporter on his side? And was not our queen sent back the next morning, unharmed, to her husband, while the Egyptian, revering the site that you have stained with the blood of your countrymen, and terrified by nocturnal visions, fled, bestowing silver and gold upon the Hebrews, beloved of God?

Shall I pass over in silence or speak of the migration of our fathers to Egypt? Lorded over by, and cowering under, kings of alien birth for four hundred years, did they not, when they might have vindicated their cause with their weapons and their hands, commit themselves to God?

Who has not heard that Egypt was overun by every species of wild beast and wasted with every disease; that their land yielded no fruit, the Nile failed; that the ten plagues followed one after the other; and that in consequence, our fathers were sent forth under escort, without bloodshed and without danger, God conducting them as the future guardians of His temple?

Did not Philistia, and the idol Dagon, groan under the ravage of our holy ark, carried off by the Syrians? Did not the entire nation of those who had removed it rue the deed, until, ulcerated in their loins and their very bowels come down with the food they ate, they, with the hands that stole it, brought it back to the sound of cymbals and timbrels, and with all manner of expiations propitiating the sanctuary? It was God who then led our fathers, because, employing neither hand nor weapon, they committed the issue to His decision.

When Sennacherib, king of the Assyrians, with all Asia in his train, encamped around this city, was it by human hands he fell? Were not those hands resting from arms and lifted in prayer while an angel of God, in one single night, destroyed that countless host? And did not the Assyrian, when he rose in the morning, find one hundred and eight-five thousand dead, and with the remnant flee from the Hebrews, who were neither armed nor in pursuit?

You have heard, moreover, of the captivity in Babylon, where our people passed seventy years in exile and did not shake off the yoke and recover their liberty until Cyrus granted it in gratitude to God. They were accordingly sent forth by him and re-established the temple-worship of their Ally. In short, there is no instance of our ancestors having triumphed by arms or failed of success without them when they committed their cause to God. When they remained within their own borders, they conquered, as seemed good to their Judge; when they took the field, they were invariably defeated.

Thus, when the king of Babylon laid siege to this city, Zedekiah, our sovereign, having, contrary to the prophetic warnings of Jeremiah, given him battle, was himself taken prisoner and saw the city and the Temple leveled to the ground. Yet, how much more moderate was that prince than your rulers, and his subjects, than you! For though Jeremiah proclaimed aloud that they were hateful to God for their transgressions and would be carried away captive if they did not surrender the city, neither the king nor the people put him to death. But you, to pass over what you have done within the city—for I am unable adequately to describe your enormities—heap abuses on me who exhort you to save yourselves and assail me with missiles, exasperated at being reminded of your misdeeds and not brooking even the mention of those crimes that you daily perpetrate.

Again, when our ancestors went forth in arms against Antiochus, surnamed Epiphanes, who was then besieging the city and who had been guilty of many outrages against the Deity, they were cut to pieces in the battle, the city was plundered by the enemy, and the sanctuary left desolate three years and six months.

Need I cite still more examples? Who enlisted the Romans against our country? Was it not the impiety of its inhabitants? Whence did our servitude arise? Was it not from a sedition of our forefathers when the madness of Aristobulus [II] and Hyrcanus [II] and their mutual quarrels brought Pompey against the city, and God subjected to the Romans those who were unworthy of liberty? Accordingly, after a siege of three months they surrendered, though they had not sinned against the laws and the sanctuary so grievously as you and though they possessed much greater resources for war.

And do we not know the fate of Antigonus, the son of Aristobulus [II], in whose reign God again punished the people for their transgressions by the capture of the city where Herod, son of Antipater, brought upon us Sosius, Sosius the Roman army, by whom they were shut up in siege for six months, until in retribution for their sins they were captured and the city plundered by the enemy?

Thus it appears that arms have never been granted to our nation; to war is to incur inevitable disaster. For, doubtless, it is the duty of those who inhabit holy ground to commit all to divine disposal, and when they seek to conciliate the Judge on high, to scorn the aid of human hands. But as for you, what have you done that has been blessed by our lawgiver [Moses]? Or what have you left undone that has been condemned by him? How much more impious are you than those who were more speedily subdued! You have disdained no secret sins—thefts, I mean, and treacherous plots against men, and adulteries—while in rapine and murders you vie with each other and cut for yourselves new and strange paths of wickedness. The Temple has become a receptable for all, and this divine place—which even the Romans from afar revered, forgoing many of their own customs in deference to our law—has been polluted by native hands. And do you after all this expect Him, thus impiously treated, to be your ally? Verily, ye are righteous suppliants, and pure are the hands with which you appeal to your Defender! Did our king lift up such hands in prayer against the king of Assyria [Sennacherib] when in one single night God destroyed that mighty host! And do the Romans commit such wickedness as did the king of Assyria that you may hope for like vengeance upon them? Did not he accept money from our sovereign on condition that he would spare the city, and then come down, in violation of his oaths, to burn the sanctuary? Whereas the Romans ask but the customary tribute that our fathers paid to theirs. Obtaining this, they will neither destroy the city nor touch the holy things. They concede to you everything else—the freedom of your families, the security of your property, and the preservation of the sacred laws. It is madness, then, to expect that God should accord the same treatment to the just as to the unjust.

But, further, He knows how to inflict immediate vengeance, when necessary. Thus, He broke the Assyrians on the very first night of their encampment. And thus, had he judged our generation worthy of freedom, or the Romans of punishment, He would at once, as He did with the Assyrians, have laid His hand upon them—when Pompey interfered with our nation, when, after him, Sosius came, when Vespasian ravaged Galilee, and lastly, now, when Titus was approaching Jerusalem. Yet Magnus [Pompey] and Sosius, besides sustaining no injury, took the city by assault, while Vespasian went from the war he made against us to become emperor. As for Titus, the very springs that had previously dried up for you flow more copiously for him. For prior to his arrival, as you know, Siloam and all the springs outside the city had failed, insomuch that water was sold by the *amphora*, while now they flow in such abundance for your enemies as to suffice not only for themselves and their cattle but even for the gardens. This amazing phenomenon you have experienced before, on the occasion of the capture of the city, when the aforementioned king of Babylon advanced with his army and took and burned both the city and the sanctuary even though, in my opinion, the Jews of the period were not so deeply impious as you. I cannot, therefore, but think that God has withdrawn from the holy places and taken His stand on the side of those against whom you are now in arms.

Why, since even a good man will flee from a wanton house and abhor its inmates, do you then persuade yourselves that God still remains with you in your evil course—that God who sees all secret things and hears what is buried in silence? Yet what is there buried in silence among you, or what concealed? Nay, what has not been exposed to your foes? For you make ostentatious display of your enormities and daily contend who shall be the worst, making an exhibition of your iniquity as though it were a virtue.

Nonetheless, a path of safety yet remains, if you will. The Deity is easily reconciled towards those who confess and repent. O iron-hearted men! throw away your weapons; take compassion on your country already on the point of destruction! Turn and behold the beauty of that which you are betraying. What a city! what a temple! the gifts of how many nations! Against these, would any man guide the flames? Who wishes that these should be no more? And what is more worthy of being preserved than these? Obdurate beings, and more insensible than stone! Even if you look not on these objects with the eyes of natural affection, yet at any rate pity your families, and let each of you have before his eyes children, wife, and parents, ere long to be the victims of famine and war.

I am aware that I have a mother, a wife, a family not ignoble, and an ancient and illustrious house involved in the danger; and I may perhaps be thought on their account to tender you this advice. Put them to death, take my blood as the price of your own safety; for I too am ready to die, if upon my death you learn wisdom.

Aelius Aristides: *Oration to Rome*

The Age of the Antonines was eulogized as a period of unprecedented peace and prosperity for the empire. This was pre-eminently true of the reign of Antoninus Pius (138–161 A.D.), when Roman territory was almost everywhere free from foreign war and internal strife. Provincials could be expected to be appreciative. The consummate literary expression of gratitude for these blessings is to be found in the *Oration to Rome* of Publius Aelius Aristides (ca. 117–189 A.D.). Aristides, from a noble Greek family in Mysia, was a product of the so-called "Second Sophistic," a Greek literary revival which promoted elaborate rhetoric and traveling scholars who drew large audiences and even larger salaries. Aristides was among the more successful and celebrated of these sophists. His travels brought him to Rome in the reign of Antoninus Pius. Freedom of circulation and material rewards inspired Aristides to paint a rosy picture indeed in his Roman oration, a picture which has dominated subsequent literature on the Antonine age. The security of the empire receives lavish praise: peaceful commerce in men and materials can intermingle from the ends of the earth under the protective umbrella of benevolent Roman legions. The gracious extension of Roman citizenship has erased distinctions between the humble and the mighty and has joined all men in a common enterprise. Echoes appear again of the old analysis of Rome as a mixed and balanced constitution, now spreading its system to bring freedom to all the world. The emperor provides necessary and salutary leadership at the top, guiding the fortunes of the empire in accordance with the principles of justice and equity. The slogans familiar and traditional from Polybius to Pliny find reflection in the mouth of the provincial. Aristides' tract is the classic statement of the prosperous and grateful provincial.

The following selections are from Aelius Aristides, *Roman Oration*, Secs. 10–13, 34–39, 59–66, 74–75, 90–91, 99–101, 109, trans. James H. Oliver in *The Ruling Power* (Philadelphia: The American Philosophical Society, 1953), 896–97, 899, 901–3, 905–7. Reprinted by permission of the publisher.

10. Some chronicler, speaking of Asia, asserted that one man ruled as much land as the sun passed, and his statement was not true because he placed all Africa and Europe outside the limits where the sun rises in the East and sets in the West. It has now however turned out to be true. Your possession is equal to what the sun can pass, and the sun passes over your land. Neither the Chelidonean nor the Cyanean promontories limit your empire, nor does the distance from which a horseman can reach the sea in one day, nor do you reign within fixed boundaries, nor does an-

other dictate to what point your control reaches; but the sea like a girdle lies extended, at once in the middle of the civilized world and of your hegemony.

11. Around it lie the great continents greatly sloping, ever offering to you in full measure something of their own. Whatever the seasons make grow and whatever countries and rivers and lakes and arts of Hellenes and non-Hellenes produce are brought from every land and sea, so that if one would look at all these things, he must needs behold them either by visiting the entire civilized world or by coming to this city. For whatever is grown and made among each people cannot fail to be here at all times and in abundance. And here the merchant vessels come carrying these many products from all regions in every season and even at every equinox, so that the city appears a kind of common emporium of the world.

12. Cargoes from India and, if you will, even from Arabia the Blest one can see in such numbers as to surmise that in those lands the trees will have been stripped bare and that the inhabitants of these lands, if they need anything, must come here and beg for a share of their own. Again one can see Babylonian garments and ornaments from the barbarian country beyond arriving in greater quantity and with more ease than if shippers from Naxos or from Cythnos, bearing something from those islands, had but to enter the port of Athens. Your farms are Egypt, Sicily and the civilized part of Africa.

13. Arrivals and departures by sea never cease, so that the wonder is, not that the harbor has insufficient space for merchant vessels, but that even the sea has enough, [if] it really does.

And just as Hesiod said about the ends of the Ocean, that there is a common channel where all waters have one source and destination, so there is a common channel to Rome and all meet here, trade, shipping, agriculture, metallurgy, all the arts and crafts that are or ever have been, all the things that are engendered or grow from the earth. And whatever one does not see here neither did nor does exist. And so it is not easy to decide which is greater, the superiority of this city in respect to the cities that now are or the superiority of this empire in respect to the empires that ever were.

* * *

34. But that which deserves as much wonder and admiration as all the rest together, and constant expression of gratitude both in word and action, shall now be mentioned. You who hold so vast an empire and rule it with such a firm hand and with so much unlimited power have very decidedly won a great success, which is completely your own.

36. For of all who have ever gained empire you alone rule over men who are free. Caria has not been given to Tissaphernes, nor Phrygia to Pharnabazus, nor Egypt to someone else; nor is the country said to be enslaved, as household of so-and-so, to whomsoever it has been turned over, a man himself not free. But just as those in states of one city appoint the magistrates to protect and care for the governed, so you, who conduct public business in the whole civilized world exactly as if it were one city state, appoint the governors, as is natural after elections, to protect and care for the governed, not to be slave masters over them. Therefore governor makes way for governor unobtrusively, when his time is up, and far from staying too long and disputing the land with his successor, he might easily not stay long enough even to meet him.

37. Appeals to a higher court are made with the ease of an appeal from deme to dicastery, with no greater menace for those who make them than for those who have accepted the local verdict. Therefore one might say that the men of today are ruled by the governors who are sent out, only in so far as they are content to be ruled.

38. Are not these advantages beyond the old "Free Republic" of every people? For under Government by the People it is not possible to go outside after the verdict has been given in the city's court nor even to other jurors, but, except in a city so small that it has to have jurors from out of town, one must ever be content with the local verdict . . . [deprived] undeservedly, or, as plaintiff, not getting possession even after a favorable verdict.

But now in the last instance there is another judge, a mighty one, whose comprehension no just claim ever escapes. 39. There is an abundant and beautiful equality of the humble with the great and of the obscure with the illustrious, and, above all, of the poor man with the rich and of the commoner with the noble, and the word of Hesiod comes to pass, "For he easily exalts, and the exalted he easily checks," namely this judge and princeps as the justice of the claim may lead, like a breeze in the sails of a ship, favoring and accompanying, not the rich man more, the poor man less, but benefiting equally whomsover it meets.

*   *   *

59. But there is that which very decidedly deserves as much attention and admiration now as all the rest together. I mean your magnificent citizenship with its grand conception, because there is nothing like it in the records of all mankind. Dividing into two groups all those in your empire—and with this word I have indicated the entire civilized world—you have everywhere appointed to your citizenship, or even to kinship with you, the better part of the world's talent, courage, and leadership, while the rest you recognized as a league under your hegemony.

60. Neither sea nor intervening continent are bars to citizenship, nor are Asia and Europe divided in their treatment here. In your empire all paths are open to all. No one worthy of rule or trust remains an alien, but a civil community of the World has been established as a Free Republic under one, the best, ruler and teacher of order; and all come together as into a common civic center, in order to receive each man his due.

61. What another city is to its own boundaries and territory, this city is to the boundaries and territory of the entire civilized world, as if the latter were a country district and she had been appointed common town. It might be said that this one citadel is the refuge and assembly place of all perioeci or of all who dwell in outside demes.

62. She has never failed them, but like the soil of the earth, she supports all men; and as the sea, which receives with its gulfs all the many rivers, hides them and holds them all and still, with what goes in and out, is and seems ever the same, so actually this city receives those who flow in from all the earth and has even sameness in common with the sea. The latter is not made greater by the influx of rivers, for it has been ordained by fate that with the waters flowing in, the sea maintain its volume; here no change is visible because the city is so great.

63. Let this passing comment, which the subject suggested, suffice. As we were saying, you who are "great greatly" distributed your citizenship. It was not because you stood off and refused to give a share in it to any of the others that you made your citizenship an object of wonder. On the contrary, you sought its expan-

sion as a worthy aim, and you have caused the word Roman to be the label, not of membership in a city, but of some common nationality, and this not just one among all, but one balancing all the rest. For the categories into which you now divide the world are not Hellenes and Barbarians, and it is not absurd, the distinction which you made, because you show them a citizenry more numerous, so to speak, than the entire Hellenic race. The division which you substituted is one into Romans and non-Romans. To such a degree have you expanded the name of your city.

64. Since these are the lines along which the distinction has been made, many in every city are fellow-citizens of yours no less than of their own kinsmen, though some of them have not yet seen this city. There is no need of garrisons to hold their citadels, but the men of greatest standing and influence in every city guard their own fatherlands for you. And you have a double hold upon the cities, both from here and from your fellow citizens in each.

65. No envy sets foot in the empire, for you yourselves were the first to disown envy, when you placed all opportunities in view of all and offered those who were able a chance to be not governed more than they governed in turn. Nor does hatred either steal in from those who are not chosen. For since the constitution is a universal one and, as it were, of one state, naturally your governors rule not as over the property of others but as over their own. Besides, all the masses have as a share in it the permission to [take refuge with you] from the power of the local magnates, [but there is] the indignation and punishment from you which will come upon them immediately, if they themselves dare to make any unlawful change.

66. Thus the present regime naturally suits and serves both rich and poor. No other way of life is left. There has developed in your constitution a single harmonious, all-embracing union; and what formerly seemed to be impossible has come to pass in your time: [maintenance] of control over an empire, over a vast one at that, and at the same time firmness of rule [without] unkindness.

*　　　　　*　　　　　*

74. Thus a courage like that of Hellenes and Egyptians and any others one might mention is surpassed by yours, and all, far as they are behind you in actual arms, trail still further in the conception. On the one hand you deemed it unworthy of your

rule for those from this city to be subject to the levy and to the
hardships and to enjoy no advantage from the present felicity; on
the other hand you did not put your faith in alien mercenaries.
Still you needed soldiers before the hour of crisis. So what did
you do? You found an army of your own for which the citizens
were undisturbed. This possibility was provided for you by that
plan for all the empire, according to which you count no one an
alien when you accept him for any employment where he can do
well and is then needed.

75. Who then have been assembled and how? Going over the
entire league, you looked about carefully for those who would
perform this liturgy, and when you found them, you released
them from the fatherland and gave them your own city, so that
they became reluctant henceforth to call themselves by their original ethnics. Having made them fellow-citizens, you made them also
soldiers, so that the men from this city would not be subject to
the levy, and those performing military service would none the
less be citizens, who together with their enrollment in the army
had lost their own cities but from that very day had become your
fellow-citizens and defenders.

*   *   *

90. It appears to me that in this state you have established a
constitution not at all like any of those among the rest of mankind.
Formerly there seemed to be three constitutions in human society.
Two were tyranny and oligarchy, or kingship and aristocracy,
since they were known under two names each according to the
view one took in interpreting the character of the men in control.
A third category was known as democracy whether the leadership
was good or bad. The cities had received one or the other constitution as choice or chance prevailed for each. Your state, on the
other hand, is quite dissimilar; it is such a form of government as
if it were a mixture of all the constitutions without the bad aspects
of any one. That is why precisely this form of constitution has
prevailed. So when one looks at the strength of the People and
sees how easily they get all that they want and ask, he will deem
it a complete democracy except for the faults of democracy. When
he looks at the Senate sitting as a council and keeping the magistracies, he will think that there is no aristocracy more perfect than
this. When he looks at the Ephor and Prytanis, who presides over

all of these, him from whom it is possible for the People to get what they want and for the Few to have the magistracies and power, he will see in this one, the One who holds the most perfect monarchic rule, One without a share in the vices of a tyrant and One elevated above even kingly dignity.

91. It is not strange that you alone made these distinctions and discoveries how to govern both in the world and in the city itself. For you alone are rulers, so to speak, according to nature. Those others who preceded you established an arbitrary, tyrannical rule. They became masters and slaves of each other in turn, and as rulers they were a spurious crew. They succeeded each other as if advancing to the position in a ball game. Macedonians had a period of enslavement to Persians, Persians to Medes, Medes to Assyrians, but as long as men have known you, all have known you as rulers. Since you were free right from the start and had begun the game as it were in the rulers' position, you equipped yourselves with all that was helpful for the position of rulers, and you invented a new constitution such as no one ever had before, and you prescribed for all things fixed rules and fixed periods.

*　　　　*　　　　*

99. Cities gleam with radiance and charm, and the whole earth has been beautified like a garden. Smoke rising from plains and fire signals for friend and foe have disappeared, as if a breath had blown them away, beyond land and sea. Every charming spectacle and an infinite number of festal games have been introduced instead. Thus like an ever-burning sacred fire the celebration never ends, but moves around from time to time and people to people, always somewhere, a demonstration justified by the way all men have fared. Thus it is right to pity only those outside your hegemony, if indeed there are any, because they lose such blessings.

100. It is you again who have best proved the general assertion, that Earth is mother of all and common fatherland. Now indeed it is possible for Hellene or non-Hellene, with or without his property, to travel wherever he will, easily, just as if passing from fatherland to fatherland. Neither Cilician Gates nor narrow sandy approaches to Egypt through Arab country, nor inaccessible mountains, nor immense stretches of river, nor inhospitable tribes of barbarians cause terror, but for security it suffices to be a Roman citizen, or rather to be one of those united under your hegemony.

101. Homer said, "Earth common of all," and you have made it come true. You have measured and recorded the land of the entire civilized world; you have spanned the rivers with all kinds of bridges and hewn highways through the mountains and filled the barren stretches with posting stations; you have accustomed all areas to a settled and orderly way of life. Therefore, I see on reflection that what is held to be the life before Triptolemus is really the life before your time,—a hard and boorish life, not far removed from that of the wild mountains. Though the citizens of Athens began the civilized life of today, this life in its turn has been firmly established by you, who came later but who, men say, are better.

＊   ＊   ＊

109. Let all the gods and the children of the gods be invoked to grant that this empire and this city flourish forever and never cease until stones [float] upon the sea and trees cease to put forth shoots in spring, and that the great governor and his sons be preserved and obtain blessings for all.

My bold attempt is finished. Now is the time to register your decision whether for better or for worse.

Acts of the Pagan Martyrs

Josephus' apologia for Rome and Aelius Aristides' lofty encomium of the empire represent the sort of works which would naturally be fostered and promoted by the government. They evinced the proper image of Roman rule. Opponents and rebels would have a more dangerous and difficult task in public dissemination of their views. Hence, documents from the dissenters are scanty. But traces remain of an "underground" literature from Alexandria, the so-called *Acts of the Pagan Martyrs*. Alexandria was a center of immigration. A Greek city from its inception, it saw a large influx of Jews and endured supervision from Roman governors. The Greek aristocracy in the city evolved a bitter resentment for the Jewish community and an even greater hatred for Rome, which tolerated Jewish claims and offended the sensibilities of Greek leaders. The *Acts of the Pagan Martyrs*, as presently preserved, are scrappy papyrus fragments. But they reflect a larger compilation, over several generations, of anti-Roman stories and martyr tales of Alexandrine leaders who supported the Greek cause and suffered at the hands of Roman emperors. No one can vouch for the accuracy of the historical detail contained in these narratives. The important element is the dissemination of anti-Roman propaganda in the East. The selections included here are some of the larger fragments from the collection, dating from the first and second centuries A.D. The first records the trial of Isidorus and Lampon before the Emperor Claudius; in the second, Trajan judges a dispute between Greek and Jewish envoys from Alexandria; and the final fragment gives the execution of Appian at the hands of the Emperor Commodus, son of Marcus Aurelius. Common themes are readily detectable: the tyrannical character of the emperors, who pander to the Jews and pervert justice; the courageous defiance of Roman power by Greek champions.

The following selections are from *The Acts of the Pagan Martyrs*, trans. H. A. Musurillo (London: Oxford University Press, 1954), 24–26, 47–48, 69–70. Reprinted by permission of The Clarendon Press.

The Alexandrian envoys were summoned and the emperor postponed their hearing until the following day. The fifth day of Pachon, in the [thirteenth?] year of Claudius Caesar Augustus. . . .

The sixth day of Pachon: the second day. Claudius Caesar hears the case of Isidorus, gymnasiarch of Alexandria, *v.* King Agrippa in the . . . gardens. With him sat twenty senators (and in addition to these) sixteen men of consular rank, the women of the court also attending . . . Isidorus' trial.

Isidorus was the first to speak: My Lord Caesar, I beseech you to listen to my account of my native city's sufferings.

THE EMPEROR: I shall grant you this day.

All the senators who were sitting as assessors agreed with this, knowing the kind of man Isidorus was.

CLAUDIUS CAESAR: Say nothing . . . against my friend. You have already done away with two of my friends, Theon the exegete and . . . .

LAMPON to ISIDORUS: I have looked upon death . . . .

CLAUDIUS CAESAR: Isidorus, you have killed many friends of mine.

ISIDORUS: I merely obeyed the orders of the emperor at the time. So too I should be willing to denounce anyone *you* wish.

CLAUDIUS CAESAR: Isidorus, are you really the son of an actress?

ISIDORUS: I am neither slave nor actress's son, but gymnasiarch of the glorious city of Alexandria. But you are the cast-off son of the Jewess Salome! And therefore . . .

LAMPON said to ISIDORUS: We might as well give in to a crazy Emperor.

CLAUDIUS CAESAR: Those whom I told (to carry out) the execution of Isidorus and Lampon . . . .

. . . in the . . . gardens. With him sat twenty senators, sixteen men of consular rank, women of the court also attending . . . Isidorus' trial.

ISIDORUS began by saying: My Lord Caesar, I beseech you to hear my account of my native city's sufferings.

THE EMPEROR: I grant you this day.

All the senators who were sitting as assessors agreed with this, knowing the kind of man Isidorus was.

CLAUDIUS CAESAR: Say nothing . . . against my friend. You have already done away with two of my friends, Theon the exegete and Naevius, prefect of Egypt and prefect of the pretorian guard at Rome; and now you prosecute this man.

ISIDORUS: My Lord Caesar, what do you care for a twopenny-halfpenny Jew like Agrippa?

CLAUDIUS CAESAR: What? You are the most insolent of men to speak. . . .

ISIDORUS: My Lord Augustus, with regard to your interests, Balbillus indeed speaks well. But to you, Agrippa, I wish to retort in connexion with the points you bring up about the Jews. I accuse them of wishing to stir up the entire world. . . . We must consider the entire mass. They are not of the same temperament as the Alexandrians, but live rather after the fashion of the Egyptians. Are they not on a level with those who pay the poll-tax?

AGRIPPA: The Egyptians have had taxes levied on them by their rulers. . . . But no one has levied taxes on the Jews.

BALBILLUS: Look to what extremes of insolence either his god or . . .

*   *   *

. . . Dionysius, who had held many procuratorships, and Salvius, Julius Salvius, Timagenes, Pastor the gymnasiarch, Julius Phanias, Philoxenus the gymnasiarch-elect, Sotion the gymnasiarch, Theon, Athenodorus, and Paulus of Tyre, who offered his services as advocate for the Alexandrians. When the Jews learned this, they too elected envoys from their own group, and thus were chosen Simon, Glaucon, Theudes, Onias, Colon, Jacob, with Sopatros of Antioch as their advocate. They set sail, then, from the city, each party taking along its own gods, the Alexandrians (a bust of Serapis, the Jews . . .).

. . . He conversed with their companions; and when the winter was over they arrived at Rome. The emperor learned that the Jewish and Alexandrian envoys had arrived, and he appointed the day on which he would hear both parties. And Plotina approached [?] the senators in order that they might oppose the Alexandrians and support the Jews. Now the Jews, who were the first to enter, greeted Emperor Trajan, and the emperor returned their greeting most cordially, having already been won over by Plotina. After them the Alexandrian envoys entered and greeted the emperor. He, however, did not go to meet them, but said:

"You say 'hail' to me as though you deserved to receive a greeting—after what you have dared to do to the Jews! . . ."

[TRAJAN:] You must be eager to die, having such contempt for death as to answer even me with insolence.

HERMAISCUS said: Why, it grieves us to see your Privy Council filled with impious Jews.

CAESAR said: This is the second time I am telling you, Hermaiscus: you are answering me insolently, taking advantage of your birth.

HERMAISCUS said: What do you mean, I answer you insolently, greatest emperor? Explain this to me.

CAESAR said: Pretending that my Council is filled with Jews.

HERMAISCUS: So, then, the word "Jew" is offensive to you? In that case you rather ought to help your own people and not play the advocate for the impious Jews.

As Hermaiscus was saying this, the bust of Serapis that they carried suddenly broke into a sweat, and Trajan was astounded when he saw it. And soon tumultuous crowds gathered in Rome and numerous shouts rang forth, and everyone began to flee to the highest parts of the hills. . . .

*   *   *

APPIAN: . . . who sending the wheat [?] to the other cities, sell it at four times its price, so as to recover their expenses.

THE EMPEROR said: And who receives this money?

APPIAN said: You do.

THE EMPEROR: Are you certain of this?

APPIAN: No, but that is what we have heard.

THE EMPEROR: You ought not to have circulated the story without being certain of it. [I say,] executioner!

As Appian was being taken off to execution he noticed a dead body and said: "Ah, dead one, when I go to my country, I shall tell Heraclianus my father and . . ." And while he was saying this, turning around he saw Heliodorus and said: "Have you nothing to say, Heliodorus, at my being led to execution?"

HELIODORUS said: To whom can we speak, if we have no one who will listen? On, my son, go to your death. Yours shall be the glory of dying for your dearest native city. Be not distressed; . . .

The emperor [then] recalled Appian. The emperor said: "Now you know whom you are speaking to, don't you?"

APPIAN: Yes, I do: Appian speaks to a tyrant.
THE EMPEROR: No, to an emperor.
APPIAN: Say not so! Your father, the divine Antoninus, was fit to be emperor. For, look you, first of all he was a philosopher; secondly, he was not avaricious; thirdly, he was good. But you have precisely the opposite qualities: you are tyrannical, dishonest, crude!

Caesar [then] ordered him to be led away to execution. As Appian was being taken, he said: "Grant me but one thing, my Lord Caesar."

THE EMPEROR: What?
APPIAN: Grant that I may be executed in my noble insignia.
THE EMPEROR: Granted.

Appian [then] took his fillet and put it on his head, and putting his white shoes on his feet, he cried out in the middle of Rome: "Come up, Romans, and see a unique spectacle, an Alexandrian gymnasiarch and ambassador led to execution!"
The evocatus immediately ran back and reported this to the emperor, saying: "Do you sit idle, my Lord, while the Romans murmur in complaint?"

THE EMPEROR: What are they complaining about?
THE CONSUL: About the execution of the Alexandrian.
THE EMPEROR: Have him brought back.

When Appian had come in, he said: "Who is it this time that called me back as I was about to greet Death again and those who died before me, Theon and Isidorus and Lampon? Was it the Senate or you, you brigand-chief?"

THE EMPEROR: Appian, I am accustomed to chasten those who rave and have lost all sense of shame. You speak only so long as I permit you to.

APPIAN: By your *genius*, I am neither mad nor have I lost my sense of shame. I am making an appeal on behalf of my noble rank and my privileges.

THE EMPEROR: How so?

APPIAN: As one of noble rank and a gymnasiarch.

THE EMPEROR: Do you suggest that I am not of noble rank?

APPIAN: That I know not; I am merely appealing on behalf of my own nobility and privileges.

THE EMPEROR: Do you not know then that . . . ?

APPIAN: If you are really not informed on this matter, I shall tell you. To begin with, Caesar saved Cleopatra . . . [and then he] got control of the empire and, as some say borrowed . . . .

The *Sibylline Oracles*

For the Greeks of Alexandria anti-Semitism and anti-Romanism went hand in hand. Roman favoritism toward the Jews aroused the fury of the Alexandrines. But it does not follow that all Jews welcomed the hegemony of Rome. Many of Josephus' countrymen found his Roman sympathies obnoxious, as can be discerned in the *Sibylline Oracles*. The credentials of the Sibyl went back to early antiquity. Prior to the founding of the Republic, so tradition had it, the oracle was already established in Rome. It was consulted for many centuries thereafter by Roman statesmen and diplomats for prognostications of the future. The Sibylline responses were carefully collected and compiled for ready consultation. That canon has now perished. But enemies of Rome could now appropriate the form for their own purposes. From the first century A.D. on, Hellenized Jews and, later, the Christians constructed their own "Sibylline Books," putting in the mouth of the pagan oracle denunciations of paganism itself, harsh attacks on Rome, and predictions of the fall of the Roman empire. The fourth book of the *Sibylline Oracles* was evidently composed by Jews in the latter years of the first century A.D. It is a revealing example of anti-Roman propaganda in the era of the Flavians, contemporary with the very different attitude of the Romanized Jew Josephus. The Sibyl proclaims herself as no longer the mouthpiece of pagan gods, but of the sole true God. The ways of Rome are denounced and condemned. There follows an historical sketch of the rise and fall of ancient empires, given, of course, in the form of a prophecy. Rome's arrogance and brutality are evidenced particularly by the sack of Jerusalem, a reference to the great Jewish war under Vespasian. But the heart of the oracular pronouncement concerns the fate of Rome. Divine judgment lies in store. A violent end will come from on high, raining terror and destruction upon the faithless, before a new restoration wipes away the traces of Rome's empire. The intensity of Jewish bitterness has no better documentation than this selection.

The following selection is from the *Sibylline Oracles*, Book IV, trans. Rev. H. N. Bate in *The Sibylline Oracles, Books III–V* (London: The Society for Promoting Christian Knowledge; New York: The Macmillan Company, 1918), 83–92. Reprinted by permission of the publishers.

Hear, ye people of proud Asia and Europe, all the true prophecies which I shall utter with honeyed mouth from our shrine; no oracular voice am I of false Phœbus, whom vain men called a god, and falsely reckoned as a seer, but of the great God, not fashioned by hands of men in the likeness of dumb idols graven in stone. He hath not for His habitation a stone dragged into a temple, deaf and dumb, a bane and a woe to mortals; but one which may not be seen from earth nor measured by mortal eyes, nor was fashioned by mortal hand: He who beholdeth all things together, and Himself is seen of none: in whose hand are dark night and day, the sun and the moon and the sea where go the fish, the earth and the rivers and unfailing streams, things created for life, rain giving birth to the fruit of the field, and to trees, the vine and the olive. It is He who has smitten through my mind with a scourge, that I should declare unerringly to men all that now is and shall be hereafter from the first generation to the tenth; for He shall try every word as He brings it to pass. But thou, O people, give ear in all things to the Sibyl, as she pours forth the stream of truth from holy lips.

Happy among men shall they be upon earth who love to bless the great God before taking food and drink, trusting in the ways of godliness: who shall turn away their eyes from every temple and all altars, vain structures of stones that cannot hear, defiled with the blood of living things and sacrifices of four-footed beasts; and will have an eye to the glory of the one God, doing no presumptuous deeds of blood nor trafficking for thievish gain— abominable are such works—having no base desires for strange women [nor for defilement with men, loathly and hateful], whose ways and manners and piety other men will not follow, so shameless is their desire, but they will mock at them with scorn and laughter, and in their witlessness will miscall them fools—so evil and presumptuous are their own works. Faithless is the whole race of men. But when the judgement of the world and of mortals shall come which God shall make, judging the godly and ungodly alike, then shall He send the godless away into darkness [and then shall they know what impiety they have done], but the godly shall continue upon the grain-giving earth, and God will give them breath and life and grace. But this shall all come to pass in the tenth generation; now will I speak of that which shall be from the first generation.

First the Assyrians shall rule over all mankind, holding sway and rule over the world for six generations, from the day when in the wrath of the God of heaven He caused a flood to break forth, and overwhelmed the earth with its cities and all that dwelt therein.

Them the Medes shall subdue, and hold the throne in pride; two generations only are theirs, in which these happenings shall be: there shall be dark night at the midnoon of day; the stars shall fall from heaven, and the orb of the moon, and the earth shall be shaken with the noise of a great earthquake, and lay low many cities and works of men, and islands shall rise out of the depths of the sea.

But when great Euphrates runs high with blood, then shall the dread cry of war be raised between Mede and Persian; the Persians shall fall beneath the spear of the Medes and fly beyond the great water of Tigris. And the Persian power shall be the greatest in all the world, yet for them is appointed but one generation of wealth and rule.

Then shall deeds be done such as men would pray God to avert, warfare and murder, dissensions, flight, burning of towers and overturning of cities, when proud Hellas shall sail against the broad Hellespont, bringing grievous doom to Phrygia and to Asia.

But upon Egypt and her broad plough-lands of wheat shall come dearth and lean harvests for the course of twenty years, when the Nile that nurtures the blade shall hide elsewhere beneath the earth his dark water.

From Asia a king shall come, lifting up a mighty sword, in countless ships, walking on the wet ways of the sea, and cutting through a high-peaked mountain in his voyaging; him trembling Asia shall receive back, as he flees for refuge from the war.

Sicily, unhappy isle, a great river of fire shall burn up, as Etna vomits out its flame; and Croton, that great city, shall fall into a deep abyss.

Hellas shall have strife; raging against each other they shall lay low many cities, and many lives shall they destroy in their fighting; but the strife shall be of doubtful issue to either side.

But when the race of men reaches the tenth generation, the yoke of slavery, with fear, shall fall upon the Persians.

But when the Macedonians hold the proud sceptre, thereafter shall Thebes suffer misery and capture. Carians shall inhabit Tyre, and the Tyrians shall perish. Samos, banks of sand shall cover it all, and Delos shall no more answer its name, but be wholly deleted. Babylon, great to behold but small in fight, shall stand fortified with hopes that profit nothing. Bactra the Macedonians shall inhabit, and they who are subject to Bactra and Susa shall all flee into the land of Hellas.

The day shall yet come, when Pyramus with his silver stream shall throw up a bar of sand as far as the holy island. And thou, Baris, shalt fall, and Cyzicus, when the earth is violently shaken, and cities collapse. Upon the Rhodians shall come the last, but the greatest evil.

Neither shall Macedonia keep her power; but from the west a great war shall grow up against her from Italy, whereby the whole world shall be made subject, enslaved under the yoke of the sons of Italy.

And thou, poor Corinth, shalt see the day of thy capture. Carthage, thy towers too shall bow the knee to the ground.

Hapless Laodicea, thee shall an earthquake lay low in ruin, but thou shalt stand again as a city with foundations. Fair Myra of Lycia, never shall the earth, when once it is shaken, give thee firm standing; thou shalt fall headlong to the ground, and pray to find another land of refuge, as a sojourner, when in thunderings and earthquake the dark water of the sea spreads sand over Patara, for their godlessness.

Thee too, Armenia, oppression and slavery awaits.

To the men of Jerusalem also shall come an evil storm-blast of war from Italy, and shall lay waste the great temple of God, when putting their trust in folly they shall cast away godliness and do hateful deeds of blood before the temple; and then shall a great king from Italy flee away like a deserter, unseen, unheard of, beyond the ford of Euphrates, after he has polluted his hands with the hateful murder of his mother, doing the deed with wicked hand. And many round his throne shall drench the soil of Rome with their blood, when he has fled beyond the land of Parthia.

To Syria shall come a Roman chieftain, who shall burn with fire the temple of Jerusalem, slay many of the Jews, and lay in ruin that great land of broad fields.

Then shall an earthquake destroy both Salamis and Paphos, when the dark water shall break over Cyprus, the sea-girt isle.

But when from a cleft in the earth, in the land of Italy, a flame of fire shoots out its light to the broad heaven, to burn up many cities and slay their men, and a great cloud of fiery ashes shall fill the air, and sparks fiery red shall fall from heaven, then should men know the wrath of the God of heaven, because they destroyed the blameless people of the godly. Then shall come to the west the strife of war stirred up, and the exiled man of Rome, lifting up a mighty sword, crossing the Euphrates with many tens of thousands.

Hapless Antioch, they shall no more call thee a city, when through thy foolishness thou fallest beneath the spear; pestilence shall then lay waste Syria, and the dread cry of battle.

Ah, wretched Cyprus, thee the spreading wave of the sea shall overwhelm, and the fierce storms of winter shall drive over thee.

Great wealth shall come to Asia, which Rome herself had made spoil of, and had stored in her rich houses; twice as much shall she then repay to Asia, and war shall restore it with interest.

The citadels of the Carians by the waters of Mæander, all the fair citadels they had fortified, bitter famine shall waste them, when the dark water of Mæander overwhelms them.

But when the faith of godliness has perished from among men, and righteousness is no more seen in the world . . . and living in unholy deeds they deal violently, doing evil with presumption, and none takes account of the godly, but in their great folly and unwisdom they destroy them all, rejoicing in violence, and staining their hands in blood; then shall they know that God is no longer merciful, but that gnashing His teeth in anger He will destroy the whole race of men at once with a great burning.

Wretched mortals, repent ye of these things, and provoke not the great God to shew all His anger; put away your swords, the slaying of men with groanings, and your deeds of violence, wash your bodies from head to foot in running streams, and lift up your hands to heaven, asking forgiveness for the deeds done aforetime, and make propitiation with gifts for your impiety; God will give repentance and will not destroy: He will cease from His anger, if ye all practice godliness in your minds, and hold it precious. But if ye will not hearken to me in your folly, but love impiety and give no good hearing to all these things, there shall be fire over the whole earth and a great sign of a sword with a trumpet, at the rising of the sun: and all the earth shall hear loud wailing and a mighty noise. It shall burn up the whole earth and destroy the whole race of men, all cities and rivers, with the sea: and it shall consume all things, and they shall be dust of fire.

But when all is turned to dust and ashes, and God who kindled it shall put to sleep the mighty fire, God Himself shall clothe the bones and ashes again in human shape, and re-make men as they were before. And then shall be the judgement, in which God himself shall judge the world again; all that sinned in godlessness, over them shall earth be heaped to cover them, dark spaces of Tartarus and Stygian recesses of Gehenna. But all that are godly, they shall live again on the earth, and God shall give them breath and life and grace, even to the godly; and all shall then look upon themselves, beholding the sweet light of a sun that never sets; most blessed shall he be who shall live to see that time.

Tacitus: *The Histories*

The complex intermingling of pro- and anti-Roman sentiments is best exemplified in the turbulent nation of the Gauls. Divisions and tribal rivalries were endemic in Gaul. When Julius Caesar first brought Roman arms into the area he found many tribes willing to cooperate with Rome rather than to join forces with their countrymen. These varied attitudes persisted in succeeding generations. The emperor Tiberius was faced with a Gallic rebellion but could reckon on the loyalty of other Gauls. Claudius introduced Gallic chieftains into the Roman senate, but Nero's rapacious governors stirred resentment again. When the Julio-Claudian dynasty tottered and Rome was engulfed in civil war in 68 A.D., Gaul rose in arms again, but her warriors engaged on both sides and against one another. In 70 A.D. the Batavian leader Civilis sought to exploit the situation. The Batavians dwelled astride the lower Rhine near the North Sea. Allies of Rome, they were impatient with unequal treatment and hoped to raise revolt on both sides of the Rhine. The speech put into Civilis' mouth by Tacitus in his *Histories* is an argument designed to stir German and Gaul alike, by stressing common grievances and imposing unity in revolt. Roman rule means conscription for Roman purposes; imperial legates are concerned only for plunder and spoil; ally and subject are treated alike in common slavery to the conqueror. But Tacitus can present equally cogent arguments on the other side. The Roman general Cerealis addresses the Gauls and expounds the advantages of cooperation with the imperial power. Even if the Roman yoke is at times oppressive, the drawbacks are outweighed by the benefits. Rome alone can settle the ruinous internal strife in Gaul; Rome promotes Gallic leaders to positions of responsibility in the empire; liberty is but a deceptive catchword and in no way preferable to the peace and stability of imperial rule. The balanced account deliberately obscures Tacitus' own leanings. But a hint exists in the typically Tacitean innuendo contained in the last line of the selection.

The following selections are from Tacitus, *Histories*, Book IV, Secs. 14, 17, 73–74, trans. Moses Hadas in Moses Hadas, ed., *The Complete Works of Tacitus* (New York: The Modern Library, 1942), 601–4, 646–47. Copyright 1942 by Random House, Inc. Reprinted by permission of Random House, Inc. and Alfred A. Knopf, Inc.

14. Civilis, who was resolved on rebellion, and intended, while concealing his ulterior designs, to reveal his other plans as occasion presented itself, set about the work of revolution in this way. By command of Vitellius all the Batavian youth was then being summoned to the conscription, a thing naturally vexatious, and which the officials made yet more burdensome by their rapacity and profligacy, while they selected aged and infirm persons, whom they might discharge for a consideration, and mere striplings, but of distinguished beauty (and many attain even in boyhood to a noble stature), whom they dragged off for infamous purposes. This caused indignation, and the ringleaders of the concerted rebellion prevailed upon the people to refuse the conscription. Civilis collected at one of the sacred groves, ostensibly for a banquet, the chiefs of the nation and the boldest spirits of the lower class. When he saw them warmed with the festivities of the night, he began by speaking of the renown and glory of their race, and then counted the wrongs and the oppressions which they endured, and all the other evils of slavery. "There is," he said,

no alliance, as once there was; we are treated as slaves. When does even a legate come among us, though he come only with a burdensome retinue and in all the haughtiness of power? We are handed over to prefects and centurions, and when they are glutted with our spoils and our blood, then they are changed, and new receptacles for plunder, new terms for spoliation, are discovered. Now the conscription is at hand, tearing, we may say, for ever children from parents, and brothers from brothers. Never has the power of Rome been more depressed. In the winter quarters of the legions there is nothing but property to plunder and a few old men. Only dare to look up, and cease to tremble at the empty names of legions. For we have a vast force of horse and foot; we have the Germans our kinsmen; we have Gaul bent on the same objects. Even to the Roman people this war will not be displeasing; if defeated, we shall still reckon it a service to Vespasian, and for success no account need be rendered.

*   *   *

17. For the moment this was a brilliant success, and it had its use for the future. They possessed themselves of some arms and some vessels, both of which they wanted, while they became very famous throughout Germany as the champions of liberty. The tribes of Germany immediately sent envoys with offers of troops. The co-operation of Gaul Civilis endeavoured to secure by politic liberality, sending back to their respective states the captured prefects of cohorts, and giving permission to their men to go or stay as they preferred. He offered to those who stayed service on honourable terms, to those who departed the spoils of the Roman army. At the same time he reminded them in confidential conversations of the wrongs which they had endured for so many years, while they falsely gave to a wretched slavery the name of peace. "The Batavians," he said,

> though free of tribute, have yet taken up arms against our common masters. In the first conflict the soldiers of Rome have been routed and vanquished. What will be the result if Gaul throws off the yoke? What strength is there yet left in Italy? It is by the blood of the provinces that the provinces are conquered. Think not of how it fared with the armies of Vindex. It was by Batavian cavalry that the Ædui and the Arverni were trampled down, and among the auxiliaries of Verginius there were found Belgian troops. To those who will estimate the matter aright it is evident that Gaul fell by her own strength. But now all are on the same side, and we have whatever remnants of military vigour still flourished in the camps of Rome. With us too are the veteran cohorts to which the legions of Otho lately succumbed. Let Syria, Asia Minor, and the East, habituated as it is to despotism, submit to slavery; there are many yet alive in Gaul who were born before the days of tribute. It was only lately indeed that Quintilius Varus was slain, and slavery driven out of Germany. And the Emperor who was challenged by that war was not a Vitellius, but a Caesar Augustus. Freedom is a gift bestowed by nature even on the dumb animals. Courage is the peculiar excellence of man, and the Gods help the braver side. Let us then, who are free to act and vigorous, fall on a distracted and exhausted enemy. While some are supporting Vespasian, and others Vitellius, opportunities are opening up for acting against both.

*　　　　*　　　　*

73. Cerialis then convoked an assembly of the Treveri and Lingones, and thus addressed them:

I have never cultivated eloquence; it is by my sword that I have asserted the excellence of the Roman people. Since, however, words have very great weight with you, since you estimate good and evil, not according to their real value, but according to the representations of seditious men, I have resolved to say a few words, which, as the war is at an end, it may be useful for you to have heard rather than for me to have spoken. Roman generals and Emperors entered your territory, as they did the rest of Gaul, with no ambitious purposes, but at the solicitation of your ancestors, who were wearied to the last extremity by intestine strife, while the Germans, whom they had summoned to their help, had imposed their yoke alike on friend and foe. How many battles we have fought against the Cimbri and Teutones, at the cost of what hardships to our armies, and with what result we have waged our German wars, is perfectly well known. It was not to defend Italy that we occupied the borders of the Rhine, but to insure that no second Ariovistus should seize the empire of Gaul. Do you fancy yourselves to be dearer in the eyes of Civilis and the Batavi and the Transrhenane tribes, than your fathers and grandfathers were to their ancestors? There have ever been the same causes at work to make the Germans cross over into Gaul, lust, avarice, and the longing for a new home, prompting them to leave their own marshes and deserts, and to possess themselves of this most fertile soil and of you its inhabitants. Liberty, indeed, and the like specious names are their pretexts; but never did any man seek to enslave his fellows and secure dominion for himself, without using the very same words.

74. Gaul always had its petty kingdoms and intestine wars, till you submitted to our authority. We, though so often provoked, have used the right of conquest to burden you only with the cost of maintaining peace. For the tranquillity of nations cannot be preserved without armies; armies cannot exist without pay; pay cannot be furnished without tribute; all else is common between us. You often command our legions. You rule these and other provinces. There is no privilege, no exclusion. From worthy Emperors you derive equal advantage, though you dwell so far away, while cruel rulers are most formidable to their neighbours. Endure the passions and rapacity of your masters, just as you bear barren seasons and excessive rains and other natural evils. There will be vices as long as there are men. But they are not perpetual, and they are compensated by the occurrence of better things. Perhaps, however, you expect a milder rule under Tutor and Classicus, and fancy that armies to repel the Germans and the Britons will be furnished by less tribute than you now pay. Should the Romans be driven out (which God forbid) what can result but wars between all these nations? By the prosperity

and order of eight hundred years has this fabric of empire been consolidated, nor can it be overthrown without destroying those who overthrow it. Yours will be the worst peril, for you have gold and wealth, and these are the chief incentives to war. Give therefore your love and respect to the cause of peace, and to that capital in which we, conquerors and conquered, claim an equal right. Let the lessons of fortune in both its forms teach you not to prefer rebellion and ruin to submission and safety.

With words to this effect he quieted and encouraged his audience, who feared harsher treatment.

Part Six

THE FADED IDEAL

The Roman empire fell on evil days after the age of the Antonines. Years of anarchy and violence in the third century had devastating and irreversible consequences. The quality of the rulers was part of the story. Roman emperors—once men of stature, power, and an aura of being larger than life—were now ephemeral creatures, succeeding one another to the throne of Rome in a depressing series of incompetent or helpless characters. For every new emperor there seemed to be two or three pretenders to the crown proclaimed by various legions in scattered parts of the empire. Nor was it internal strife alone which featured those dismal years. Struggles among Romans, weakness, and confusion opened the gates to barbarian tribes who ringed the frontiers, poised for an opening, for plunder, and for *Lebensraum*. To Rome's traditional enemies, the Germans on the Rhine and Upper Danube, were added the Dacians, the Goths, and the Persians. Roman arms carried less and less authority. To the provincial populations of the empire Rome no longer possessed the drawing power she once had. The signs of decentralization were everywhere present. When men were in peril of their lives and property almost constantly, their loyalties moved swiftly and naturally to the nearest strong man who could offer protection. Roman military personnel were drawn more and more from the frontier provinces; these were men who possessed Roman citizenship but to whom "Rome" meant only the security of their property, not some distant city in Italy which they had never seen and were never likely to see. Ferment within and invasions without greatly enhanced Germanic influence in the empire. The transplantation of increasing numbers of Germans to Roman soil as free farmers in the third century foreshadowed the ultimate emergence of the medieval Romano-German states.

The prolonged crisis had telling repercussions on the economic situation. As military difficulties increased and legions were drawn to the peripheries on a more permanent basis, the economic demands naturally increased in those areas, as did the means to meet them. The process of decentralization was irreversible. Local loyalties centered on municipalities, provincial territories, and military colonies rather than on Rome. Aristocrats with landed estates abroad stopped going to Rome even to attend the senate; peasants who were recruited into the armies fought only to preserve their own properties. Taxation was rapidly increased while taxable resources were shrinking. Business activity was gradually coming to a standstill. Plagues, invasions, and civil wars drastically reduced the population. Financial burdens on the provincials were crippling. Countless numbers must have been ruined and reduced to poverty. Others could escape only by flight and brigandage.

Strong action came from the top in the late third and early fourth centuries. The emperors Diocletian and Constantine imposed more rigid controls and a tightened regimen. The army received reorganization and the frontiers enjoyed more careful protection. But basic changes loosed in the previous century could not be arrested. The fragility of the empire had been exposed. The future lay with units smaller than the empire—and with Christianity.

Ammianus Marcellinus: *History*

It will not cause surprise to learn that literature languished in a depressing era. Insofar as there was vigor and novelty it was largely the monopoly of Christian writers. Their verdicts on the course of Roman history and the nature of pagan society were, naturally, sharply hostile. The Christian historians

Lactantius and Eusebius stressed Roman brutality and the triumph of Christianity over her persecutors. Churchmen like St. Ambrose, St. Jerome, and John Chrysostom denounced Roman character, the luxury and vice of the pagan world which precipitated its downfall. That approach culminated in St. Augustine's massive *City of God,* which set the fall of Rome in a context of human history marked by pagan sin and self-destruction.

Christian attacks on Roman morals and the conduct of empire are abundant. But it is more striking and revealing to find these attacks in the historian Ammianus Marcellinus (ca. 330–393 A.D.). Ammianus' pagan credentials are impeccable. Born at Antioch, a center of Greek culture, he served in the armies of Rome, wrote for Roman audiences in Latin, and heaped praise on the pagan emperor Julian. Ammianus wrote a history of Rome from 96 A.D. (where Tacitus left off) to his own day. The earlier portions are lost, but the history of his contemporary age, the fullest part of his work, is preserved. Ammianus' judgment is clear. The Roman aristocracy is infected with luxury, idleness, greed, and hypocrisy; the commons is addicted to boorishness, stupidity, and gluttony. The life of the mind is neglected and shunned; men interest themselves only in the games, in food, and in prostitutes. Even more telling are Ammianus' comments on the course of Roman "justice." They supply a useful corrective to the usual homage paid by textbooks to the glories of Roman law. Ammianus exposes the low quality of barristers and judges, the venality and sham that dominate the courtroom, the entanglements and nonsense that pervert the judicial process. The verdict of the historian is devastating. It is a fitting epilogue on the faded ideal.

The following selections are from Ammianus Marcellinus, *History,* Book XIV, Ch. 6, Secs. 2–26; Book XXVIII, Ch. 4, Secs. 6–34; Book XXX, Ch. 4, Secs. 1–22; trans. John C. Rolfe in *Ammianus Marcellinus,* I (Cambridge, Mass: Harvard University Press, 1956), 37–53, and *Ammianus Marcellinus,* III (Cambridge, Mass: Harvard University Press, 1958), 141–161, 319–35. Reprinted by permission of the publishers and *The Loeb Classical Library.*

2. Now I think that some foreigners who will perhaps read this work (if I shall be so fortunate) may wonder why it is

that when the narrative turns to the description of what goes on at Rome, I tell of nothing save dissensions, taverns, and other similar vulgarities. Accordingly, I shall briefly touch upon the reasons, intending nowhere to depart intentionally from the truth.

3. At the time when Rome first began to rise into a position of world-wide splendour, destined to live so long as men shall exist, in order that she might grow to a towering stature, Virtue and Fortune, ordinarily at variance, formed a pact of eternal peace; for if either one of them had failed her, Rome had not come to complete supremacy.

4. Her people, from the very cradle to the end of their childhood, a period of about three hundred years, carried on wars about her walls. Then, entering upon adult life, after many toilsome wars, they crossed the Alps and the sea. Grown to youth and manhood, from every region which the vast globe includes, they brought back laurels and triumphs. And now, declining into old age, and often owing victory to its name alone, it has come to a quieter period of life.

5. Thus the venerable city, after humbling the proud necks of savage nations, and making laws, the everlasting foundations and moorings of liberty, like a thrifty parent, wise and wealthy, has entrusted the management of her inheritance to the Caesars, as to her children.

6. And although for some time the tribes have been inactive and the centuries at peace, and there are no contests for votes but the tranquillity of Numa's time has returned, yet throughout all regions and parts of the earth she is accepted as mistress and queen; everywhere the white hair of the senators and their authority are revered and the name of the Roman people is respected and honoured.

7. But this magnificence and splendour of the assemblies is marred by the rude worthlessness of a few, who do not consider where they were born, but, as if licence were granted to vice, descend to sin and wantonness. For as the lyric poet Simonides tells us, one who is going to live happy and in accord with perfect reason ought above all else to have a glorious fatherland.

8. Some of these men eagerly strive for statues, thinking that by them they can be made immortal, as if they would gain a greater reward from senseless brazen images than from the consciousness of honourable and virtuous conduct. And they take pains to have

them overlaid with gold, a fashion first introduced by Acilius Gla-
brio, after his skill and his arms had overcome King Antiochus.
But how noble it is, scorning these slight and trivial honours, to
aim to tread the long and steep ascent to true glory, as the bard of
Ascra expresses it, is made clear by Cato the Censor. For when he
was asked why he alone among many did not have a statue, he
replied: "I would rather that good men should wonder why I did
not deserve one than (which is much worse) should mutter 'Why
was he given one?' "

9. Other men, taking great pride in coaches higher than common and in ostentatious finery of apparel, sweat under heavy
cloaks, which they fasten about their necks and bind around their
very throats, while the air blows through them because of the
excessive lightness of the material; and they lift them up with both
hands and wave them with many gestures, especially with their
left hands, in order that the over-long fringes and the tunics embroidered with party-coloured threads in multiform figures of
animals may be conspicuous.

10. Others, though no one questions them, assume a grave expression and greatly exaggerate their wealth, doubling the annual
yield of their fields, well cultivated (as they think), of which they
assert that they possess a great number from the rising to the setting sun; they are clearly unaware that their forefathers, through
whom the greatness of Rome was so far flung, gained renown, not
by riches, but by fierce wars, and not differing from the common
soldiers in wealth, mode of life, or simplicity of attire, overcame
all obstacles by valour.

11. For that reason the eminent Valerius Publicola was buried
by a contribution of money, and through the aid of her husband's
friend the needy wife of Regulus and her children were supported.
And the daughter of Scipio received her dowry from the public
treasury, since the nobles blushed to look upon the beauty of this
marriageable maiden long unsought because of the absence of a
father of modest means.

12. But now-a-days, if as a stranger of good position you enter for
the first time to pay your respects to some man who is well-to-do
and therefore puffed up, at first you will be greeted as if you were
an eagerly expected friend, and after being asked many questions
and forced to lie, you will wonder, since the man never saw you
before, that a great personage should pay such marked attention

to your humble self as to make you regret, because of such special kindness, that you did not see Rome ten years earlier.

13. When, encouraged by this affability, you make the same call on the following day, you will hang about unknown and unexpected, while the man who the day before urged you to call again counts up his clients, wondering who you are or whence you came. But when you are at last recognized and admitted to his friendship, if you devote yourself to calling upon him for three years without interruption, then are away for the same number of days, and return to go through with a similar course, you will not be asked where you were, and unless you abandon the quest in sorrow, you will waste your whole life to no purpose in paying court to the blockhead.

14. And when, after a sufficient interval of time, the preparation of those tedious and unwholesome banquets begins, or the distribution of the customary doles, it is debated with anxious deliberation whether it will be suitable to invite a stranger, with the exception of those to whom a return of hospitality is due; and if, after full and mature deliberation, the decision is in the affirmative, the man who is invited is one who watches all night before the house of the charioteers, or who is a professional dicer, or who pretends to the knowledge of certain secrets.

15. For they avoid learned and serious people as unlucky and useless, in addition to which the announcers of names, who are wont to traffic in these and similar favours, on receiving a bribe, admit to the doles and the dinners obscure and low-born intruders.

16. But I pass over the gluttonous banquets and the various allurements of pleasures, lest I should go too far, and I shall pass to the fact that certain persons hasten without fear of danger through the broad streets of the city and over the upturned stones of the pavements as if they were driving post-horses with hoofs of fire (as the saying is), dragging after them armies of slaves like bands of brigands and not leaving even Sannio at home, as the comic writer says. And many matrons, imitating them, rush about through all quarters of the city with covered heads and in closed litters.

17. And as skilful directors of battles place in the van dense throngs of brave soldiers, then light-armed troops, after them the javelin-throwers, and last of all the reserve forces, to enter the action in case chances makes it needful, just so those who have charge of a city household, made conspicuous by wands grasped in

their right hands, carefully and diligently draw up the array; then, as if the signal had been given in camp, close to the front of the carriage all the weavers march; next to these the blackened service of the kitchen, then all the rest of the slaves without distinction, accompanied by the idle plebeians of the neighbourhood; finally, the throng of eunuchs, beginning with the old men and ending with the boys, sallow and disfigured by the distorted form of their members; so that, wherever anyone goes, beholding the troops of mutilated men, he would curse the memory of that Queen Samiramis of old, who was the first of all to castrate young males, thus doing violence, as it were, to Nature and wresting her from her intended course, since she at the very beginning of life, through the primitive founts of the seed, by a kind of secret law, shows the ways to propagate posterity.

18. In consequence of this state of things, the few houses that were formerly famed for devotion to serious pursuits now teem with the sports of sluggish indolence, re-echoing to the sound of singing and the tinkling of flutes and lyres. In short, in place of the philosopher the singer is called in, and in place of the orator the teacher of stagecraft, and while the libraries are shut up forever like tombs, water-organs are manufactured and lyres as large as carriages, and flutes and instruments heavy for gesticulating actors.

19. At last we have reached such a state of baseness, that whereas not so very long ago, when there was fear of a scarcity of food, foreigners were driven neck and crop from the city, and those who practised the liberal arts (very few in number) were thrust out without a breathing space, yet the genuine attendants upon actresses of the mimes, and those who for the time pretended to be such, were kept with us, while three thousand dancing girls, without even being questioned, remained here with their choruses, and an equal number of dancing masters.

20. And, wherever you turn your eyes, you may see a throng of women with curled hair, who might, if they had married, by this time, so far as age goes, have already produced three children, sweeping the pavements with their feet to the point of weariness and whirling in rapid gyrations, while they represent the innumerable figures that the stage-plays have devised.

21. Furthermore, there is no doubt that when once upon a time Rome was the abode of all the virtues, many of the nobles detained

here foreigners of free birth by various kindly attentions, as the Lotus-eaters of Homer did by the sweetness of their fruits.

22. But now the vain arrogance of some men regards everything born outside the pomerium of our city as worthless, except the childless and unwedded; and it is beyond belief with what various kinds of obsequiousness men without children are courted at Rome.

23. And since among them, as is natural in the capital of the world, cruel disorders gain such heights that all the healing art is powerless even to mitigate them, it has been provided, as a means of safety, that no one shall visit a friend suffering from such a disease, and by a few who are more cautious another sufficiently effective remedy has been added, namely, that servants sent to inquire after the condition of a man's acquaintances who have been attacked by that disorder should not be readmitted to their masters' house until they have purified their persons by a bath. So fearful are they of a contagion seen only by the eyes of others.

24. But yet, although these precautions are so strictly observed, some men, when invited to a wedding, where gold is put into their cupped right hands, although the strength of their limbs is impaired, will run even all the way to Spoletium. Such are the habits of the nobles.

25. But of the multitude of lowest condition and greatest poverty some spend the entire night in wineshops, some lurk in the shade of the awnings of the theatres, which Catulus in his aedileship, imitating Campanian wantonness, was the first to spread, or they quarrel with one another in their games at dice, making a disgusting sound by drawing back the breath into their resounding nostrils; or, which is the favourite among all amusements, from sunrise until evening, in sunshine and in rain, they stand open-mouthed, examining minutely the good points or the defects of charioteers and their horses.

26. And it is most remarkable to see an innumerable crowd of plebeians, their minds filled with a kind of eagerness, hanging on the outcome of the chariot races. These and similar things prevent anything memorable or serious from being done in Rome. Accordingly, I must return to my subject.

*   *   *

6. And first, as often, according to the quantity of topics, I shall

give an account of the delinquencies of the nobles and then of the common people, condensing the events in a rapid digression.

7. Some men, distinguished (as they think) by famous fore-names, pride themselves beyond measure in being called Reburri, Flavonii, Pagonii, Gereones, and Dalii, along with Tarracii and Pherrasii, and many other equally fine-sounding indications of eminent ancestry.

8. Others, resplendent in silken garments, as though they were to be led to death, or as if (to speak without any evil omen) they were bringing up the rear preceded by an army, are followed by a throng of slaves drawn up in troops, amid noise and confusion.

9. When such men, each attended by fifty servants, have entered the vaulted rooms of a bath, they shout in threatening tones: "Where on earth are our attendants?" If they have learned that an unknown courtesan has suddenly appeared, some woman who has been a common prostitute of the crowd of our city, some old strumpet, they all strive to be the first to reach her, and caressing the new-comer, extol her with such disgraceful flattery as the Parthians do Samiramis, the Egyptians their Cleopatras, the Carians Artemisia, or the people of Palmyra Zenobia. And those who stoop to do such things are men in the time of whose forefathers a senator was punished with the censor's brand of infamy, if he had dared, while this was still considered unseemly, to kiss his wife in the presence of their own daughter.

10. Some of these men, when one begins to salute them breast to breast, like menacing bulls turn to one side their heads, where they should be kissed, and offer their flatterers their knees to kiss or their hands, thinking that quite enough to ensure them a happy life; and they believe that a stranger is given an abundance of all the duties of courtesy, even though the great men may perhaps be under obligation to him, if he is asked what hot baths or waters he uses, or at what house he has been put up.

11. And although they are so important and, in their own opinion, such cultivators of the virtues, if they learn that someone has announced that horses or chariots are coming from anywhere whatever, they hover over this same man and ask him questions as anxiously as their ancestors looked up to the two sons of Tyndareus, when they filled everything with joy by announcing those famous victories of olden days.

12. Their houses are frequented by idle chatterboxes, who with

various pretences of approval applaud every word of the man of loftier fortune, emulating the witty flatteries of the parasites in the comedies. For just as the parasites puff up boastful soldiers by attributing to them the sieges and battles against thousands of enemies, comparing them with the heroes of old, so these also, admiring the rows of columns hanging in the air with lofty façade, and the walls gleaming with the remarkable colours of precious stones, raise these noble men to the gods.

13. Sometimes at their banquets the scales are even called for, in order to weigh the fish, birds, and dormice that are served, whose great size they commend again and again, as hitherto unexampled, often repeating it to the weariness of those present, especially when thirty secretaries stand near by, with pen-cases and small tablets, recording these same items, so that the only thing lacking seems to be a schoolmaster.

14. Some of them hate learning as they do poison, and read with attentive care only Juvenal and Marius Maximus, in their boundless idleness handling no other books than these, for what reason it is not for my humble mind to judge.

15. Whereas, considering the greatness of their fame and of their parentage, they ought to pore over many and varied works; they ought to learn that Socrates, when condemned to death and thrown into prison, asked a musician, who was skilfully rendering a song of the lyric poet Stesichorus, that he might be taught to do this while there was still time. And when the musician asked of what use that could be to him, since he was to die on the following day, Socrates replied: "In order that I may know something more before I depart from life."

16. But a few among them are so strict in punishing offences, that if a slave is slow in bringing the hot water, they condemn him to suffer three hundred lashes; if he has intentionally killed a man, although many people insist that he be condemned to death, his master will merely cry out: "What should a worthless fellow do, notorious for wicked deeds? But if he dares to do anything else like that hereafter, he shall be punished."

17. But the height of refinement with these men at present is, that it is better for a stranger to kill any man's brother than to decline his invitation to dinner. For a senator thinks that he is suffering the loss of a rich property, if the man whom he has, after

considerable weighing of pros and cons, invited once, fails to appear at his table.

18. Some of them, if they make a longish journey to visit their estates, or to hunt by the labours of others, think that they have equalled the marches of Alexander the Great or of Caesar; or if they have sailed in their gaily-painted boats from the Lake of Avernus to Puteoli, it is the adventure of the golden fleece, especially if they should dare it in the hot season. And if amid the gilded fans flies have lighted on the silken fringes, or through a rent in the hanging curtain a little ray of sun has broken in, they lament that they were not born in the land of the Cimmerians.

19. Then when they come from the bath of Silvanus or from the healing waters of Mamaea, as any one of them emerges he has himself dried with the finest linens, opens the presses and carefully searches amongst garments shimmering with shifting light, of which he brings enough with him to clothe eleven men. At length, some are chosen and he puts them on; then he takes back his rings, which, in order that the dampness may not injure them, he has handed to a servant, and after his fingers have been as good as measured to receive them, he departs.

20. And, indeed, if any veteran has recently retired because of his years from service with the emperor, such a company of admirers attend him that . . . is considered to be the leader of the old song; the others quietly listen to what he says. He alone, like the father of a family, tells irrelevant stories and entertaining tales, and in most of them cleverly deceiving his hearers.

21. Some of these, though few in number, shrink from the name of gamblers, and therefore desire to be called rather *tesserarii*, persons who differ from each other only as much as thieves do from brigands. But this must be admitted, that while the friendships at Rome are lukewarm, those alone which are formed at the gambling table, as if they were gained by glorious toil, have a bond of union and are united by complete firmness of exceeding affection; whence some members of these companies are found to be so harmonious that you would take them for the brothers Quintilius. And so you may see a man of low station, who is skilled in the secrets of diceplaying, walking abroad like Porcius Cato after his unexpected and unlooked-for defeat for the praetorship, with a set expression of dignity and sorrow because at some great banquet or

assemblage a former proconsul was given a higher place of honour.

22. Some lie in wait for men of wealth, old or young, childless or unmarried, or even for those who have wives or children—for no distinction is observed in this respect—enticing them by wonderful trickeries to make their wills; and when they have set their last decisions in order and left some things to these men, to humour whom they have made their wills in their favour, they forthwith die; so that you would not think that the death was brought about by the working of the allotment of destiny, nor could an illness easily be proved by the testimony of witnesses; nor is the funeral of these men attended by any mourners.

23. Another, who attained some rank, moderate though it be, walking with neck puffed up, looks askance at his former acquaintances, so that you might think that a Marcellus was returning after the taking of Syracuse.

24. Many of them, who deny that there are higher powers in heaven, neither appear in public nor eat a meal nor think they can with due caution take a bath, until they have critically examined the calendar and learned where, for example, the planet Mercury is, or what degree of the constellation of the Crab the moon occupies in its course through the heavens.

25. Another, if he finds a creditor of his demanding his due with too great urgency, resorts to a charioteer who is all too ready to dare any enterprise, and causes the creditor to be charged with being a poisoner; and he is not let off until he has surrendered the bill of indebtedness and paid heavy costs. And besides, the accuser has the voluntary debtor put in prison as if he were his property, and does not set him free until he acknowledges the debt.

26. In another place a wife by hammering day and night on the same anvil—as the old proverb has it—drives her husband to make a will, and the husband insistently urges his wife to do the same. Skilled jurists are brought in on both sides, one in a bedroom, the other, his rival, in the diningroom to discuss disputed points. These are joined by opposing interpreters of horoscopes, on the one side making profuse promises of prefectures and the burial of rich matrons, on the other telling women that for their husbands' funerals now quietly approaching they must make the necessary preparations. And a maid-servant bears witness, by nature somewhat pale, . . . As Cicero says: "They know of nothing on earth

that is good unless it brings gain. Of their friends, as of their cattle, they love those best from whom they hope to get the greatest profit."

27. When these people seek any loan, you will see them in slippers like a Micon or a Laches; when they are urged to pay, they wear such lofty buskins and are so arrogant that you would think them Cresphontes and Temenus, the famous Heraclidae. So much for the senate.

28. Let us now turn to the idle and slothful commons. Among them some who have no shoes are conspicuous as though they had cultured names, such as the Messores, Statarii, Semicupae and Serapini, and Cicymbricus, with Gluturinus and Trulla, and Lucanicus with Porclaca and Salsula, and countless others.

29. These spend all their life with wine and dice, in low haunts, pleasures, and the games. Their temple, their dwelling, their assembly, and the height of all their hopes is the Circus Maximus. You may see many groups of them gathered in the fora, the crossroads, the streets, and their other meeting-places, engaged in quarrelsome arguments with one another, some (as usual) defending this, others that.

30. Among them those who have enjoyed a surfeit of life, influential through long experience, often swear by their hoary hair and wrinkles that the state cannot exist if in the coming race the charioteer whom each favours is not first to rush forth from the barriers, and fails to round the turning-point closely with his ill-omened horses.

31. And when there is such a dry rot of thoughtlessness, as soon as the longed-for day of the chariot-races begins to dawn, before the sun is yet shining clearly they all hasten in crowds to the spot at top speed, as if they would outstrip the very chariots that are to take part in the contest; and torn by their conflicting hopes about the result of the race, the greater number of them in their anxiety pass sleepless nights.

32. If from there they come to worthless theatrical pieces, any actor is hissed off the boards who has not won the favour of the low rabble with money. And if this noisy form of demonstration is lacking, they cry in imitation of the Tauric race that all strangers —on whose aid they have always depended and stood upright— ought to be driven from the city. All this in foul and absurd terms,

very different from the expressions of their interests and desires made by your commons of old, of whose many witty and happy sayings tradition tells us.

33. And it has now come to this, that in place of the lively sound of approval from men appointed to applaud, at every public show an actor of afterpieces, a beast-baiter, a charioteer, every kind of player, and the magistrates of higher and lower rank, nay even matrons, are constantly greeted with the shout "You should be these fellows' teachers!"; but what they ought to learn no one is able to explain.

34. The greater number of these gentry, given over to over-stuffing themselves with food, led by the charm of the odour of cooking and by the shrill voices of the women, like a flock of peacocks screaming with hunger, stand even from cockcrow beside the pots on tip-toe and gnaw the ends of their fingers as they wait for the dishes to cool. Others hang over the nauseous mass of half-raw meat, while it is cooking, watching it so intently that one would think that Democritus with other dissectors was examining the internal organs of dismembered animals and showing by what means future generations might be cured of internal pains.

*   *   *

1. This is what took place throughout Gaul and the northern part of the empire. But in the regions of the East, amid the profound quiet of foreign affairs, destructive internal corruption was increasing through the friends and intimates of Valens, with whom advantage prevailed over honour. For diligent efforts were exerted to turn the emperor, as a severe man and eager to hear cases at law, from his desire to act as judge; for fear that as in the times of Julian, if the defence of innocence should revive, the arrogance of powerful men, which under the licence that they had assumed was in the habit of always reaching out farther, might be checked.

2. On these and similar grounds many united in a common attempt at dissuasion and in particular the praetorian prefect Modestus, a man wholly subjected to the influence of the eunuchs of the court, of a boorish nature refined by no reading of the ancient writers. He, wearing a forced and deceptive expression, declared that the trivialities of private cases at law were beneath the dignity of the imperial majesty. Accordingly Valens, thinking that the ex-

amination of swarms of legal cases was devised to humble the loftiness of the royal power, in accordance with the advice of Modestus, abstained from it wholly, thereby opening the doors to robbery; and this grew stronger day by day through the wickedness of judges and advocates in collusion; for they sold their decisions of the cases of poor people to officers in the army, or to powerful men within the palace, and thus gained either wealth or high position.

3. This trade of forensic oratory the great Plato defined as πολιτικῆς μορίου εἴδωλον (that is, the shadow of a small part of the science of government) or as the fourth part of flattery; but Epicurus counts it among evil arts, calling it κακοτεχνία. Tisias says that it is the artist of persuasion, and Gorgias of Leontini agrees with him.

4. This art, thus defined by the men of old, the cunning of certain Orientals raised to a degree hateful to good men, for which reason it is even confined by the restraints of a time fixed beforehand. Therefore after having described in a very few words its unworthiness, with which I became acquainted while I was living in those parts, I shall return to the course of the narrative with which I began.

5. Formerly judgement-seats gained glory through the support of old-time refinement, when orators of fiery eloquence, devoted to learned studies, were eminent for talent and justice, and for the fluency and many adornments of their diction; for example Demosthenes, to hear whom, when he was going to speak, as the Attic records testify, the people were wont to flock together from all Greece; and Callistratus, to whom, when he pleaded in that celebrated case in defence of Oropos (which is a place in Euboea) that same Demosthenes attached himself, forsaking the Academy and Plato; also, Hyperides, Aeschines, Andocides, Dinarchus, and the famous Antiphon of Rhamnus, who, according to the testimony of antiquity, was the first of all to accept a fee for conducting a defence.

6. Not less eminent among the Romans were men like Rutilius, Galba, and Scaurus, conspicuous for their life, their character, and their uprightness; and later in the various epochs of their subsequent times many former censors and consuls, and men who had been honoured with triumphs, such as Crassus, Antonius, Philippus, Scaevola, and many others, after successful campaigns, after vic-

tories and trophies, distinguished themselves by civic services to the State, and winning laurels in the glorious contests of the Forum, enjoyed Fame's highest honours.

7. After these Cicero, the most eminent of them all, by the floods of his all-conquering oratory often saved the oppressed from the fiery ordeal of the courts, and declared: "It might perhaps be pardonable to refuse to defend some men, but to defend them negligently could be nothing but criminal."

8. But now it is possible to see in all the regions of the Orient powerful and rapacious classes of men flitting from one forum to another, besieging the homes of the wealthy, and like Spartan or Cretan hounds sagaciously picking up the tracks until they come to the very lairs of lawsuits.

9. Among these the first class consists of those who, by sowing the seeds of all sorts of quarrels, busy themselves with thousands of recognisances, wearing out the doors of widows and the thresholds of childless men; and if they have found even slight retreats of secret enmity, they rouse deadly hatred among discordant friends, kinsfolk, or relatives. And in these men their vices do not cool down in course of time, as do those of others, but grow stronger and stronger. Poor amid insatiable robbery, they draw the dagger of their talent to lead astray by crafty speeches the good faith of the judges, whose title is derived from justice.

10. By their persistence rashness tries to pass itself off as freedom of speech; and reckless audacity as firmness of purpose; a kind of empty flow of words as eloquence. By the perversity of these arts, as Cicero insists, it is a sin for the conscientiousness of a judge to be deceived. For he says: "And since nothing in a state ought to be so free from corruption as the suffrage and judicial decisions, I do not understand why one who corrupts them by money deserves punishment, while one who corrupts them by his eloquence is even praised. For my part, I think that he does more evil who corrupts a judge by a speech than one who does so by money; for no one can corrupt a sensible man by money, but he can do so by words."

11. A second class consists of those who profess a knowledge of law, which, however, the self-contradictory statutes have destroyed, and reticent as if they were muzzled, in never-ending silence they are like their own shadows. These men, as though revealing destinies by nativities or interpreting a Sibyl's oracles, assume a

solemn expression of severe bearing and try to make even their yawning saleable.

12. In order to seem to have a deeper knowledge of the law, they talk of Trebatius, Cascellius, and Alfenus, and of the laws of Aurunci and Sicani, which were long since forgotten and buried many ages ago along with Evander's mother. And if you pretend that you have purposely murdered *your* mother, they promise, if they have observed that you are a moneyed man, that their many recondite studies will secure an acquittal for you.

13. A third group consists of those who, in order to gain glory by their troublous profession, sharpen their venal tongues to attack the truth, and with shameless brow and base yelping often gain entrance wherever they wish. When the anxious judges are distracted by many cares, they tie up the business in an inexplicable tangle, and do their best to involve all peace and quiet in lawsuits and purposely by knotty inquisitions they deceive the courts, which, when their procedure is right, are temples of justice, when corrupted, are deceptive and hidden pits; and if anyone is deluded and falls into those pits, he will not get out except after many a term of years, when he has been sucked dry to his very marrow.

14. The fourth and last class, shameless, headstrong, and ignorant, consists of those who have broken away too soon from the elementary schools, run to and fro through the corners of the cities, thinking out mimiambic lines, rather than speeches suitable to win law-suits, wearing out the doors of the rich, and hunting for banquets and fine choice food.

15. When they have once devoted themselves to shady gain and to eagerness for money from any and every source, they urge all kinds of innocent people to involve themselves in vain litigations. And when they are allowed to defend suits, which rarely happens, amidst the very turning-points of the disputes they learn the name of their client and the purport of the business in hand from the mouth of the judge, and they so overflow with disarranged circumlocutions that in the foul hotchpotch you would think you were hearing a Thersites with his howling din.

16. But when they find themselves in the end unable to defend the charges, they turn to unbridled licence in abuse; and on this account, because of their constant insults of persons of rank, they are prosecuted and often condemned; and among them are some

who are so ignorant that they cannot remember that they ever possessed a law-book.

17. And if in a circle of learned men the name of an ancient writer happens to be mentioned, they think it is a foreign word for some fish or other edible; but if any stranger asks for the orator Marcianus (for example), who was before unknown to him, at once they all pretend that their own name is Marcianus.

18. And they no longer have before their eyes any right, but as if sold to and enslaved by avarice, they understand nothing except endless licence in making demands. And if once they have caught anyone in their nets, they entangle him in a thousand toils, purposely defaulting by pretending sicknesses one after another; and they prepare seven plausible preambles in order that the useless reading of well-known law may be introduced, thus weaving swarms of long delays.

19. And when the contending parties are stripped of everything, and days, months and years are used up, at last the case, now worn out with age, is introduced, and those brilliant principals come forth, bringing with them other shadows of advocates. And when they have come within the barriers of the court, and the fortunes or safety of some one begins to be discussed, and they ought to work to turn the sword or ruinous loss from an innocent person, the advocates on both sides wrinkling their brows and waving their arms in semblance of the gestures of actors (so that they lack only the oratorical pipe of Gracchus behind them) stand for a long time opposite each other. At last, in accordance with a pre-arranged agreement, the one who is more confident in speech utters a kind of sweet prologue, promising to emulate the ornamental language of a speech for Cluentius or Ctesiphon; and when all are wishing for the end, such is the method of his peroration that the advocates, after the semblance of a trial has gone on for three years, allege that they are not yet fully informed; and after they have obtained a further postponement, as if they had struggled with Antaeus of old, they persistently demand the pay for their danger and toil.

20. But yet, in spite of this, advocates suffer many inconveniences, not easy to be endured by a man who would live rightly. For, allured by the profits of their sedentary trade, they differ among themselves and become enemies, and they offend many by their outbursts of abusive ferocity (as has been said), which they

blab out in a torrent when they have no arguments strong enough
to fortify the weakness of the cases which have been entrusted to
them.

21. And they have to deal with judges who sometimes are taught
by the sophisms of Philistion or Aesopus, rather than reared
in the discipline of your Aristides the Just or Cato. Such men,
having bought public office for large sums of money, like tiresome
creditors prying into the resources of every kind of fortune, shake
out booty from other men's bosoms.

22. Finally, the profession of advocate has, with the rest, this
serious and dangerous evil, which is native to almost all litigants,
that although their cases may be lost by a thousand accidents,
they think their ill-success lies wholly in the ability of their advocates, and they are accustomed to attribute the outcome of every
contest to them; and they vent their anger not on the weakness
of their case or the frequent injustice of the magistrate who decides
it, but only on their defenders. But let us return to the point
from which we made the digression.

4